DOTSON

MY JOURNEY GROWING UP TRANSGENDER

GRAYSON LEE WHITE

ILLUSTRATIONS BY STEPHANIE ROTH SISSON

WEST
MARGIN
PRESS

I'd like to dedicate this book to...

Mr. K. for helping me become a good enough writer
to write this book.

My second-grade teacher (you know who you are)
for fully supporting me to be myself.

My twin sister for being my biggest ally and best friend.

Dot·son

D/o/t·S/u/n *(noun, adjective)*

1. The word you get when you combine "daughter" and "son."
2. The word I made up to describe myself before I knew the word "transgender."
3. Not the same as "tomboy," which is a girl who likes boy stuff. A Dotson is a supposed daughter who KNOWS he is really a son.

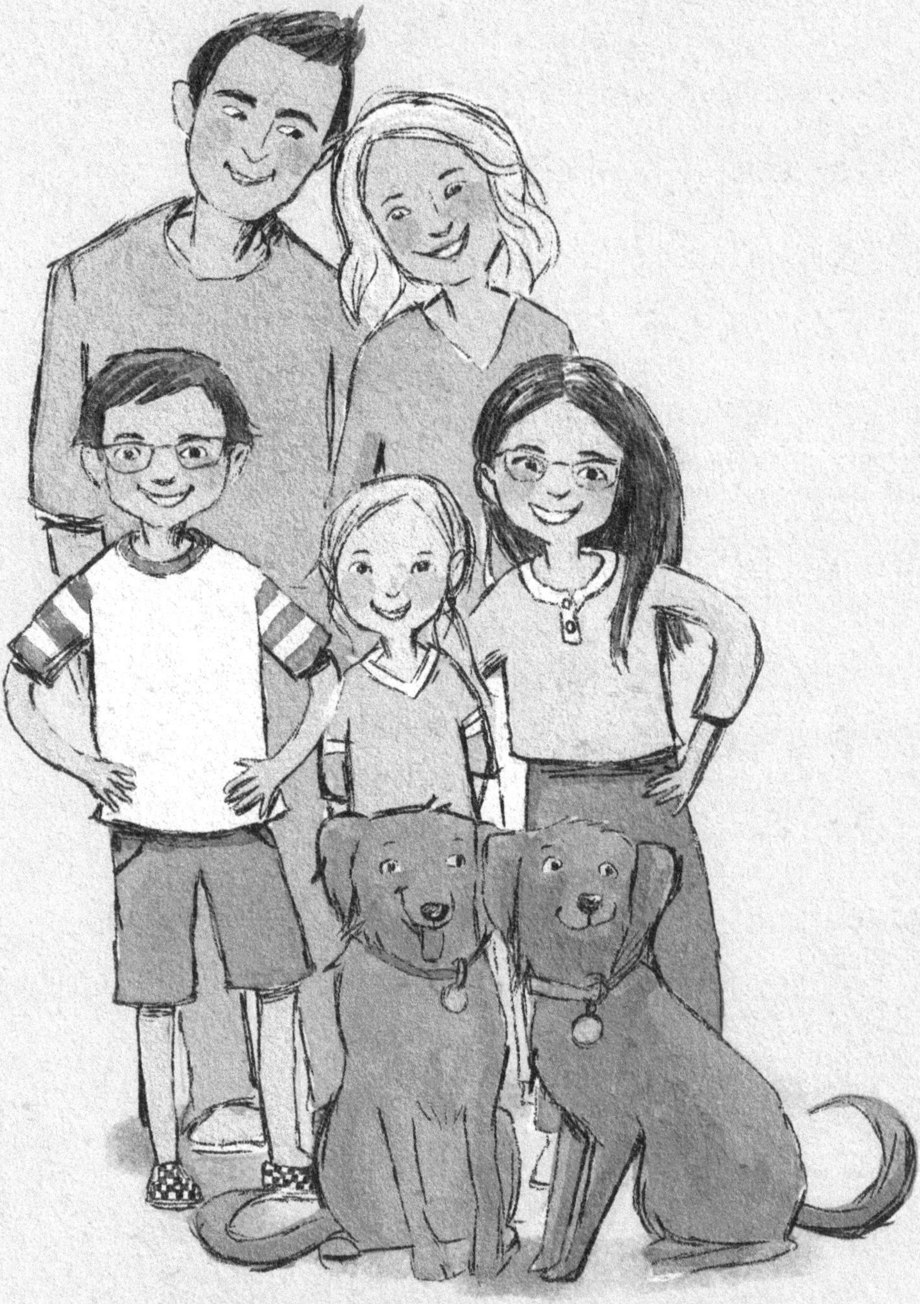

A NOTE FROM THE AUTHOR

Hey, my name is Grayson and I'm the author and, yes, the main character of *Dotson*. I live in the United States in what is considered the Midwest with my parents, my two sisters (one of which is my identical twin), and my two adorable golden retrievers.

I've known since I could barely walk that I wanted to write and publish a book someday. It looks like that someday is now—you are reading my first book! Although I'm transgender and that's an important part of my life and what this book is about, it isn't normally a big part of my personality or my writing. The stories I usually write are fantasy mixed with realistic fiction. So expect more books to come. I want to be known as a good author, not just a good trans author.

There are other things I like to do besides write, though. I recently started snowboarding and I think it's a ton of fun. I'm also learning to skateboard because I've heard it's similar to snowboarding. I think I'm going to like them both. I've played baseball and ice hockey and still enjoy going to local rinks with my family and friends in the winter.

I used to play guitar, but I got a bit out of practice during the COVID-19 quarantine. I didn't really mind being quarantined for a little bit. I'm an introvert, no question about it. But I'm not shy around the people I'm closest to. Oh, and I really like golfing with my dad and he says I'm getting pretty good at it.

One thing I've known for as long as I can remember is that I am a boy, not a girl. When people lovingly called me a "tomboy," I knew that wasn't right either. I started calling myself Dotson, a combination of "daughter" and "son." I tried to explain to my mom when I was three or four years old: "I know I'm supposed to be your daughter, but I feel more like your son. I guess I'm your... Dot-son." My mom loved the name and it stuck for a few years until we learned the correct term for what I am: transgender.

I'm really excited to share my "journey" (as my mom calls it) with you. I think "journey" makes it sound like the plot of an action movie or something when it's really just a mix of my most memorable moments and stories so far. But whatever. Either way, I hope you like it.

And if you're a trans kid, like me, I hope it helps make your life just a little bit easier.

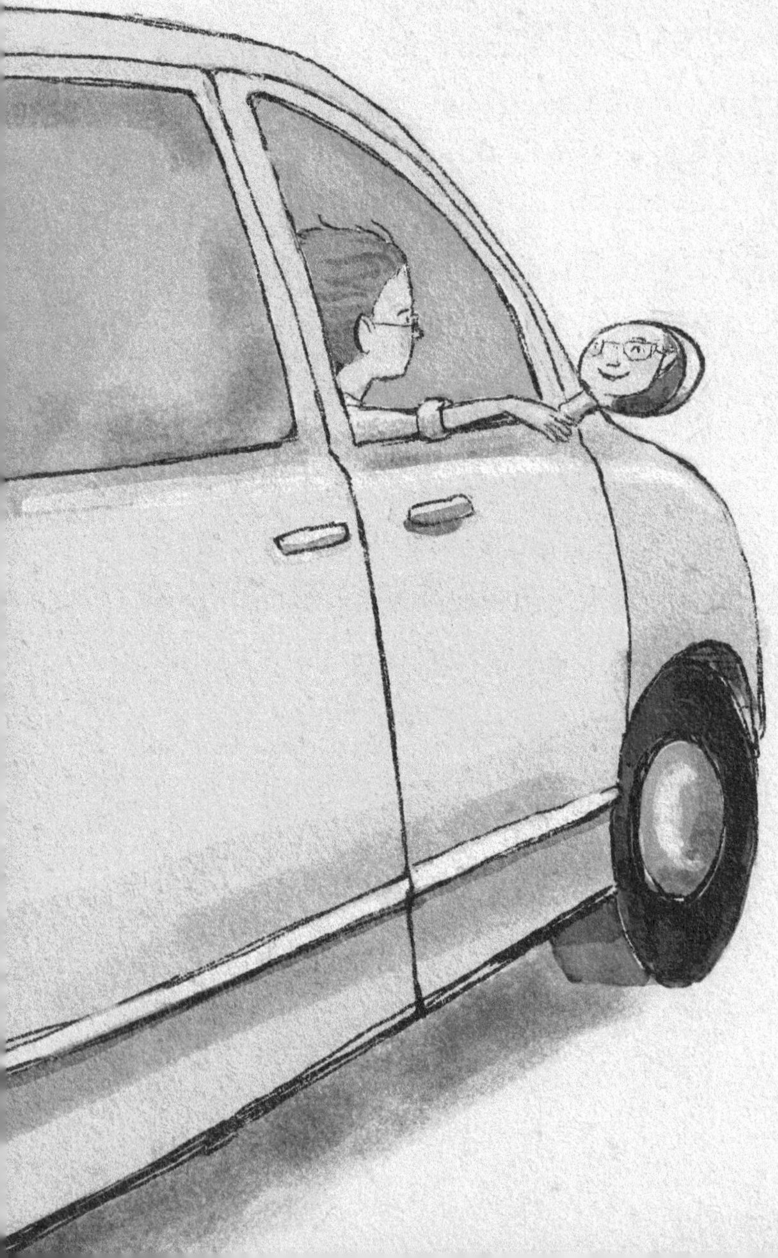

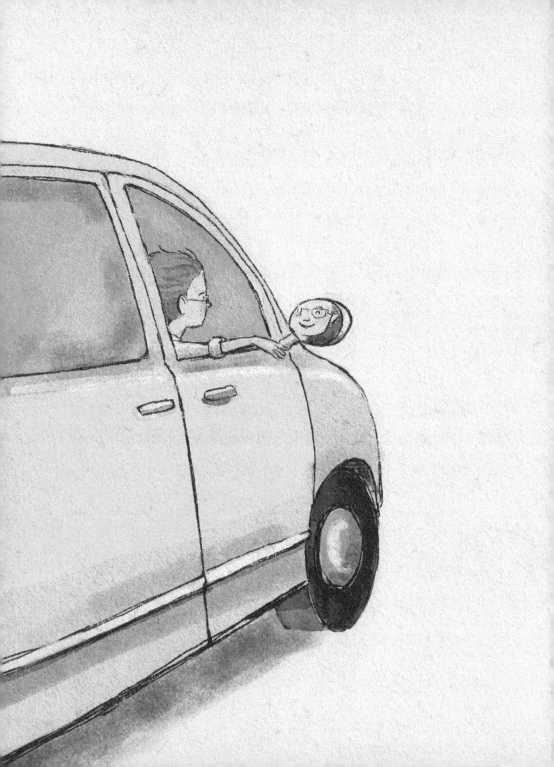

LET'S START
AT THE END
AGE 12

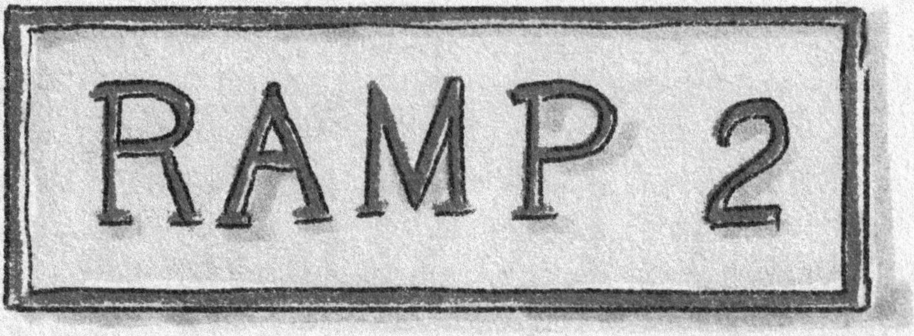
RAMP 2

It was the first day of summer, eight thirty in the morning, and I was sitting in the car instead of sleeping in. I was pretty tired because I hadn't gone to bed early the night before. Instead, I'd been at the first sleepover of the summer with two of my closest friends.

"You nervous?" my mom asked.

"Not really. I'm just excited!" I replied. She smiled.

I could see the hospital as we drove closer and closer, but of course I knew we wouldn't be inside for a couple minutes because of the annoying parking system. We finally navigated the parking ramp and walked to the elevator.

"Okay, ramp two, ramp two... don't let me forget," my mom said, stopping to let me push the elevator button.

"Ramp two. Got it, " I confirmed.

The elevator dinged and we stepped into the hospital lobby, where a nurse asked my mom questions about whether either of us had COVID-19 symptoms. After answering no over and over, they put a neon-green visitor pass on her shirt and we rode a different elevator up to floor seven.

After more sitting and more waiting in a new waiting room, a nurse took us into the doctor's office where she applied numbing cream to my leg where I would be getting the shot.

Go ahead, call me a scaredy-cat, but the numbing cream is mostly for my nerves. I used to get really panicked before any kind of shot. The numbing cream helps a lot.

Once my leg was numb, the nurse asked, "Okay, would you rather I do a countdown or just do it?"

At that moment what I was about to do felt very real. I had been waiting to start blockers (medicine that delays puberty) for most of my life.

My mind flashed back to when I was just two years old and it all started...

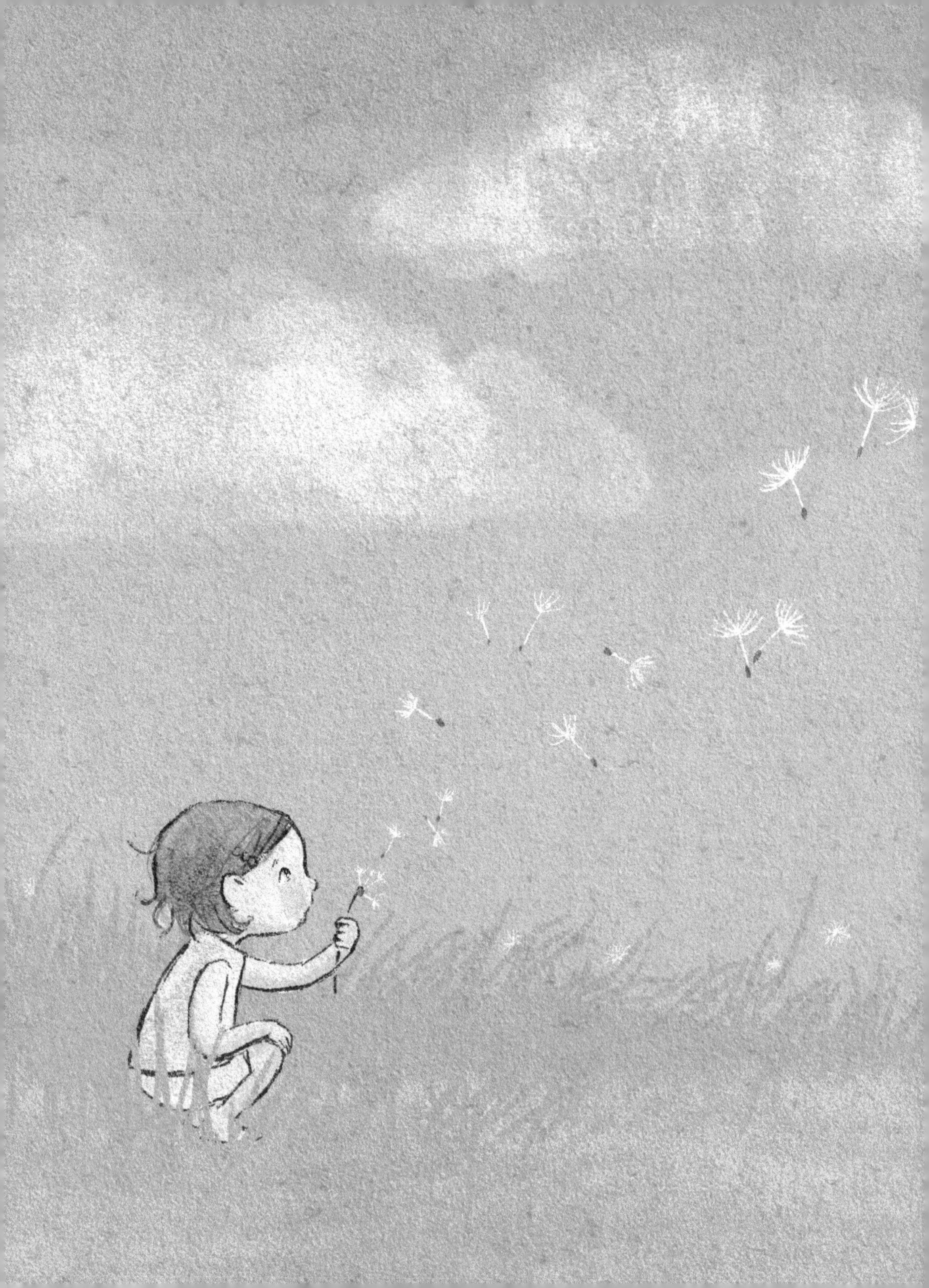

WISHES

AGE 2

"Why did God make me a girl?"

I asked my mom this as we walked back to my grandma's house from the Fourth of July bonfire. We'd been watching a big fireworks display and drawing circles with our sparklers.

"I am supposed to be a boy," I continued. "Can you ask God to make me a boy please?"

"Oh sweetie," she said, giving me a hug and kissing my forehead. "Girls are amazing and there is absolutely nothing better about boys than girls!"

Okay, I am not sure that this is exactly how it went down because I was only two, so it's hard to remember. But it's a story I've heard many, many times.

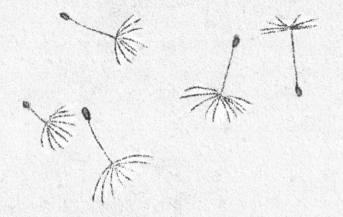

Now that I'm older, my mom tells me that she used to blame herself for not having done a good enough job making sure my sister and I knew that girls could do anything boys could do. She thought that's why I wanted to be a boy. Or because I wanted to be different from my identical twin sister.

But those were not, of course, the reasons why.

Although I can barely remember that conversation, there are a lot of things I can remember. Most kids, I think, when given a birthday cake, a puffy white dandelion, or a penny to toss into a fountain, usually wish for things. Like they might wish, "Please give me a new LEGO set," or a bike, or something along those lines.

But I never wished for toys.

Every opportunity I ever had to make a wish,
I wished for one thing. The same thing.

"Can you please make it so that I was born a boy?"
I would ask the helpless little dandelion. That was my
first wish. But the older I got, the more rational and
realistic I became.

"I wish I looked like a boy."

"I wish people called me a boy."

"I wish this whole transitioning thing will work out."

"I wish the shots wouldn't hurt."

"I wish people wouldn't be mean to me."

"I wish that someday I'll be a boy... one way or another."

I still make some of the same wishes I used to make, but a lot of them have come true. I am a boy now, legally, and in many other ways. I look like a boy. I use he/him pronouns and I have a masculine name. The shots aren't too bad (I'm just a little sore for a few days). And luckily I haven't really dealt with anyone being mean to me.

It sure seems that my last wish is well on its way.

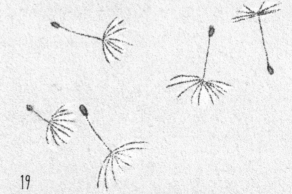

GOLF SHIRT

AGE 3½

One of the funny home videos we watch sometimes is from the Christmas right after my twin sister Gabby and I turned two. We were bouncing off the walls on Christmas morning as we opened presents. We played with our new Woody and Buzz Lightyear dolls and pedaled around the house in our matching tricycles.

"We have one more surprise for you!" Mom said.

Gabby and I ran to the large box and tore off the paper. Inside was a trunk filled with:

other girly stuff

princess dresses

shiny crowns

plastic jewelry

The video is clear—Gabby was thrilled. She dug right in, exploring everything in that magical trunk. My reaction was... well... the opposite of that. I stood shaking my head, then ran back to Woody and Buzz Lightyear.

"Hmm, not for you sweetie?" Mom asked. It didn't seem like she felt too bad that I didn't like it.

But wow, I was one rude toddler.

Fast forward to summer the following year. I can vaguely remember Dad pulling down our small suitcases and letting us pack for a trip to visit our family up north. Gabby loved it and spent lots of time carefully choosing outfits from our shared closet. Then she neatly organized piles of clothes into her pink suitcase.

Unfortunately, we didn't own many clothes that I liked. At least our parents didn't (usually) force us to dress in the same outfits like some other parents of twins. Still, most of what was hanging in our closet were dresses or rompers, and other clothes that were considered girly. I didn't like wearing any of them.

Usually when it was time to pack for trips, I would fill my suitcase with toys and then Mom or Dad would make me pick a few things to wear.

Luckily, whenever we visited my Dad's family at the lake, my cousin always let me wear his shark pajamas while I was there (I had a strange obsession with sharks—I think because they scared me), so at least I knew I wouldn't have to sleep in a nightgown.

Before one of our weekend trips up to visit our family, I had just thrown my talking Buzz Lightyear action figure into my otherwise empty suitcase when Mom and Gabby got home from the store.

"We got you a present," Mom said, reaching into her shopping bag. She pulled out a yellow polo shirt, just like the kind my dad wore golfing. It had:

a collar
buttons
a green and orange stripe

"We got it from the boys' section," Gabby announced proudly.

I threw my arms around Mom. "Thank you!" I felt like they finally understood how I had been feeling all this time. I wanted to hug Gabby too, but I didn't because I knew Mom would insist on taking a picture.

I folded my new shirt carefully and laid it neatly into my suitcase next to a pair of jeans and my sneakers.

Now I was all set.

For a couple weeks, the only things I wore were that striped golf shirt and the shark pajamas. (My cousin had eventually just let me take them home.)

But we did some shopping and slowly the amount of "boy" clothes in my closet began to grow. Soon my entire extended family knew that I didn't like dresses, skirts, or nightgowns. When someone gave me clothes for Christmas or my birthday, they were from the boys' section. After about a year, my entire wardrobe was clothes that I actually liked and didn't feel weird in.

When I was four and my sisters and I were flower "girls" at my cousin's wedding, my cousin even let me wear a tuxedo instead of the dress my sisters wore. "Thank you for letting me wear a tuxedo," I told her.

"It wouldn't feel like it was you in my wedding if you were in a dress," she replied.

It felt good that my family understood that. And while I know that not all girls wear dresses and not all boys wear pants, trust me—there's a difference in what our society considers "boy" versus "girl" clothes. From then on, I was much happier on the "boys" side of stores.

And I learned that I actually do like to pack my own suitcase when I have clothes that feel like me to put in it.

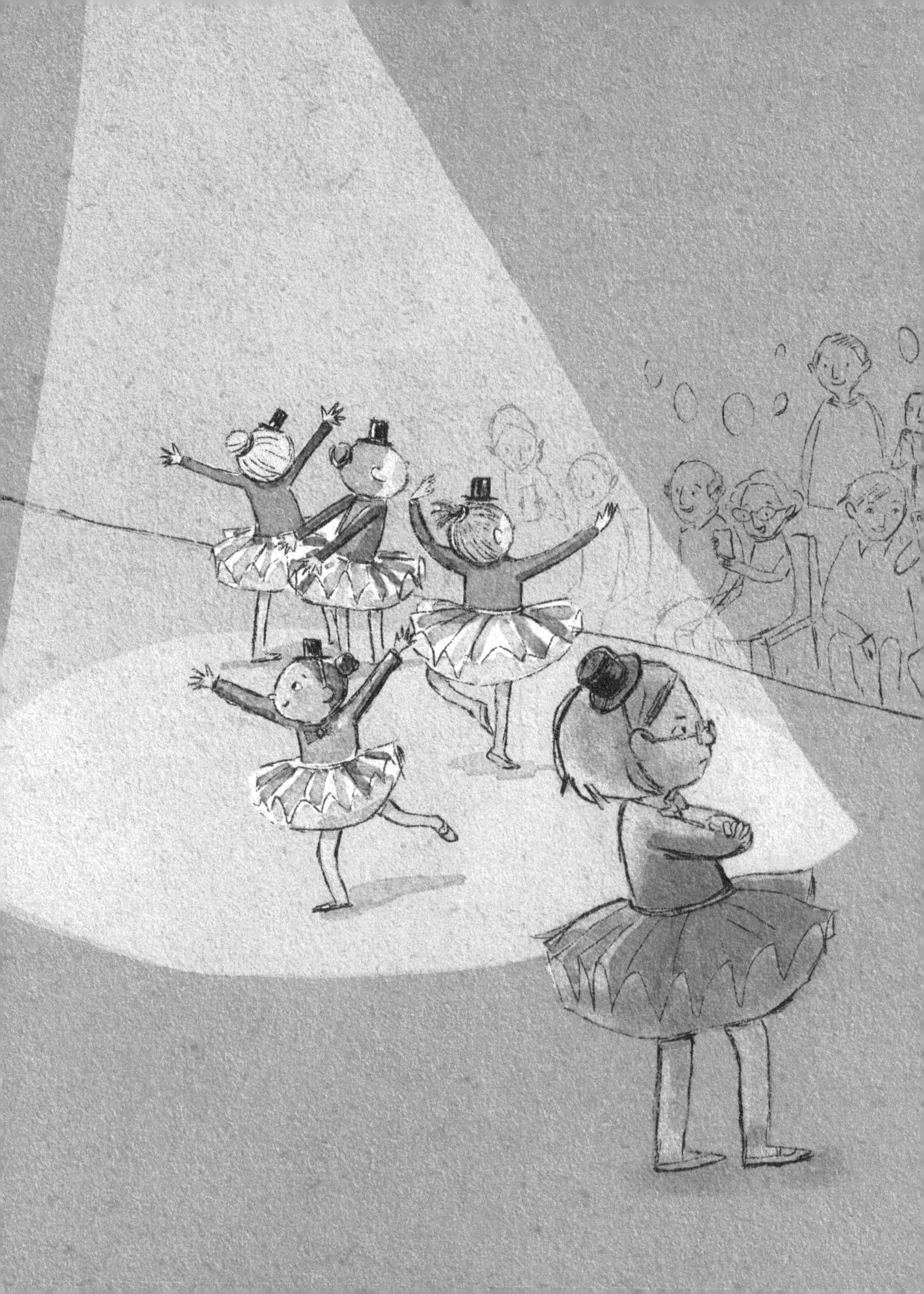

DANCE RECITAL

AGE 3½

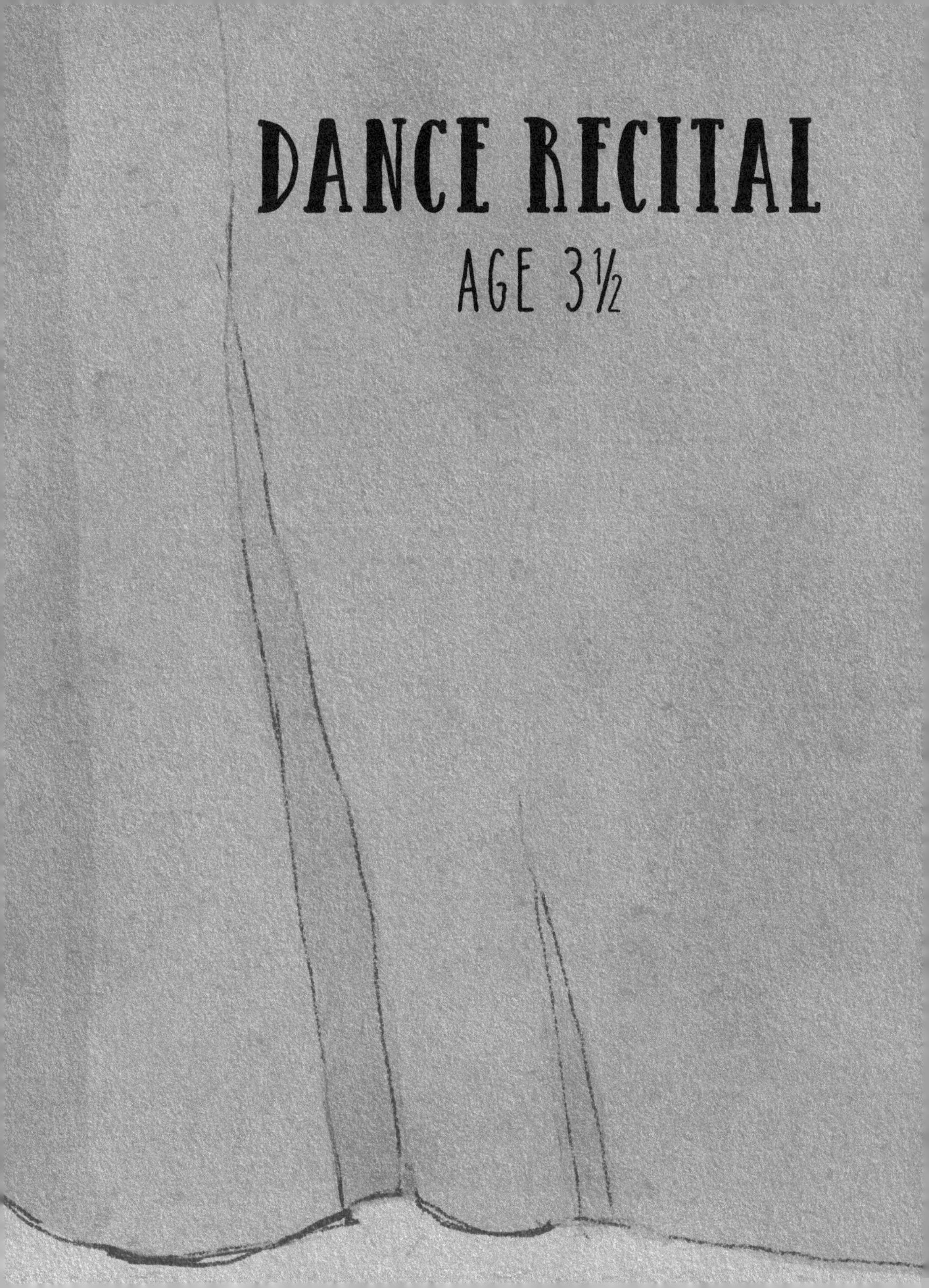

"Broadway baby, learning how to sing and dance!" the music blared.

The dance recital was beginning. My three-year-old heart was beating out of my chest as all the girls around me put their hands on their knees and rocked back and forth. I joined in (it was our first move, after all). But when I looked out into the crowd of parents and grandparents, siblings and friends, I froze.

How did I end up here, doing this silly dance in front of so many people?

Flashback to the start of the season when Gabby signed up for dance class and I did not.

"You can go today too, if you want," my mom told me as Gabby got ready.

"No thanks," I responded. Then I noticed that Gabby wasn't wearing her leotard. She was wearing an Ariel costume from *The Little Mermaid*.

"You sure?" Mom asked. "You can wear a costume this time."

The Ariel costume got me pretty excited because I had this Spider-Man costume that I looooved. Even though I'd never seen the movie, Spider-Man was (and still is) my favorite superhero. I just thought he was cool. And I would take any opportunity to wear my little red jumpsuit.

"I'll do it," I said gleefully.

When we showed up in our costumes, I noticed the other girls were wearing mostly princess costumes, so I was pretty out of place. But I wasn't embarrassed, because nobody could see me under the costume, meaning no one even knew it was me! I was in disguise, just like Spider-Man.

Dancing Spider-Man, that is.

I had a great time, so when Mom asked me later if I wanted to keep going to dance class I agreed. Every Monday, Gabby and I went to the studio. The problem was I couldn't wear my Spider-Man costume anymore. In dance class we had to wear leotards!

I wore a long-sleeved red leotard with Nike sweatpants over it.

We practiced for six or seven months, but I got sick of it and the leotards pretty quickly.

"I don't want to be in dance anymore," I whined to my mom.

"You signed up and made a commitment, so you need to stick it out until the end of this session," my mom explained, promising that I could quit after that.

Eventually, it was time for the end-of-year recital.

This time we all had to wear matching actual dance costumes (not Spider-Man costumes!) which were these sparkly black, blue, and white tuxedo things with a tutu attached! And these horribly dorky, miniature top hats we had to wear tilted to the side. It was a nightmare, for sure. But the group who danced after us was dancing to a song called "I Enjoy Being a Girl" (no kidding), so I guess I should have felt lucky.

But I didn't.

First, a whole bunch of our relatives showed up. Great—they would all see me in a tutu. Then the teachers led us onto the stage and the music started. There I was, my heart pounding, as we put our hands on our knees and rocked back and forth. Or as everyone else did, I should say. After the first two moves, I stared out at the crowd, then at us dancers. I thought about how dumb everyone looked, and I decided I wouldn't do it.

For the entire rest of the recital, I stood on the far right of the stage with my arms crossed.

I didn't dance.

I didn't move.

I didn't respond when the nice dance teachers encouraged me, "Go ahead, it'll be fine!"

I knew it wouldn't be fine and I wasn't going anywhere.

Afterward, my grandma still gave Gabby and me flowers and told us how proud she was of both of us. Nobody seemed to care that I didn't actually dance at all.

I never signed up for dance class again, but Gabby did. Occasionally I wished I had signed up for hip-hop dance class where there were more boys and they got to wear cool costumes.

At least I thought they were cool. They were pretty much just sweatpants.

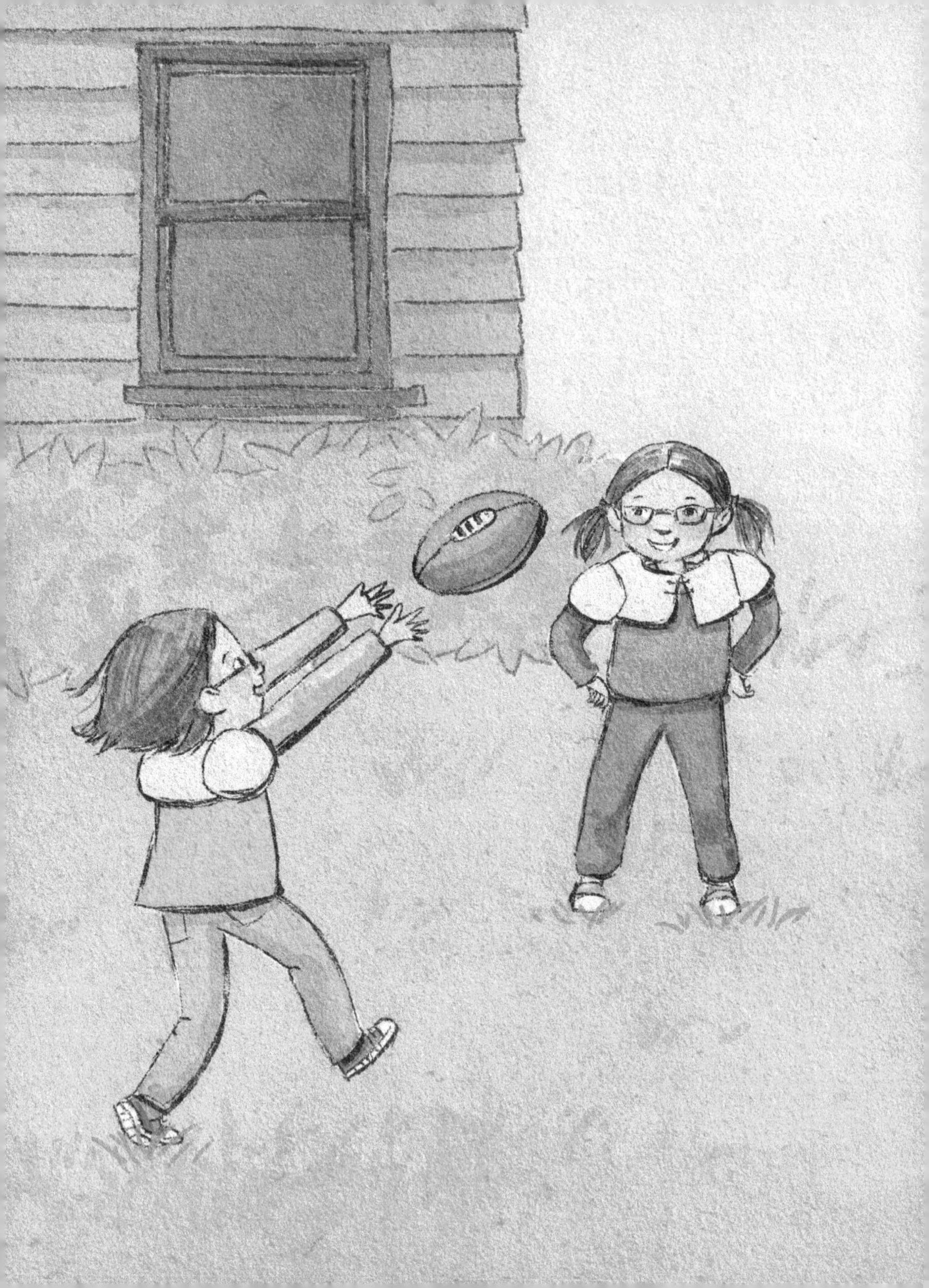

GOD DOESN'T MAKE

MISTAKES

AGE 5

"Bye!" I called to the bus driver as he drove away from my stop. I was done with school for the day. I ran to my house and dropped off my backpack.

"I'm going next door," I told Dad.

My sister Gabby and I ran to the next-door neighbor's backyard where our friends were waiting. We were playing pirates in their playhouse and sandbox.

"Everyone needs to pick a pirate name," our neighbor Rachel said.

I knew they expected me to be a girl pirate, but I didn't want to be. Playing make-believe was my one chance to be whoever I wanted to be, and I liked that.

"Can I be Luke?" I asked.

"No, you have to be a girl," Rachel said, matter-of-factly, "because that's who God made you."

I may have only been in kindergarten at the time, but that earned an eye roll from me. "If God made me who I am," I told her, "then he made me want to be a boy."

I continued on as the world's most dangerous pirate... Luke.

The next day after school we played pirates again, but this time Rachel's brothers joined and then offered to teach Gabby and me how to play football. "Put these on," they said, handing us some spare pads. The pads didn't really fit me, and I wasn't very good. But it felt pretty awesome to be able to play football like I was one of the boys.

And I was better than Gabby, which was my main goal.

Soon one of the older boys suggested we set up a game for that night and invite our parents to watch. I agreed excitedly and Gabby said she would do it too. We practiced a bit more and then the neighbors went inside to look for shirts we could wear as jerseys. Gabby and I were supposed to gather a crowd to come watch the game. Gabby went to round up Mom and Dad, and my little sister Ellie and I went to tell the neighbor's parents.

I knocked on the door of the house where I had been playing pirates in the backyard for the past two days. As I waited, I felt nervous to talk to grown-ups I didn't know very well.

All you have to do is say it, my brain told me.

I took a deep breath as their dad opened the door.

"Hi... uh... do you wanna watch us play football tonight?" I asked.

He didn't answer but just stared at me for a minute. "Why are you wearing those clothes and playing football?" he questioned. "You're a young girl. Shouldn't you be playing with makeup or putting on dresses?"

My already racing heart skipped a beat.

Should I be wearing makeup and dresses? I wondered.

No.

Even in kindergarten I knew him saying that to me didn't feel right.

The truth was that even back then I always preferred playing sports or video games over joining my sisters to play with makeup or dresses.

"Uh, no. I guess I just don't like them," I stammered, staring at my feet. "So, do you want to come watch?"

"Sure," he said, surprising me.

We played football for hours that night, until it got dark. And it was fun, I guess. My team didn't win, but oh well. My mind kept going back to what the neighbor had said to me. At bedtime that night I told my dad, "Rachel's dad told me that I'm a girl, so I should wear makeup and dresses."

"Hmm..." he said, pausing for a moment. "I guess that's his opinion. But that's not what your mom and I believe, or what you believe, right?"

I kind of knew that already, but hearing him say it was nice.

I don't think our neighbor is a bad person, but I never really liked him after that. I don't think he understood how strongly I felt that I wasn't a girl, and neither did his kids. I guess if you don't feel the way I did (and still do), it's hard to understand.

But I sure appreciate the people who at least try.

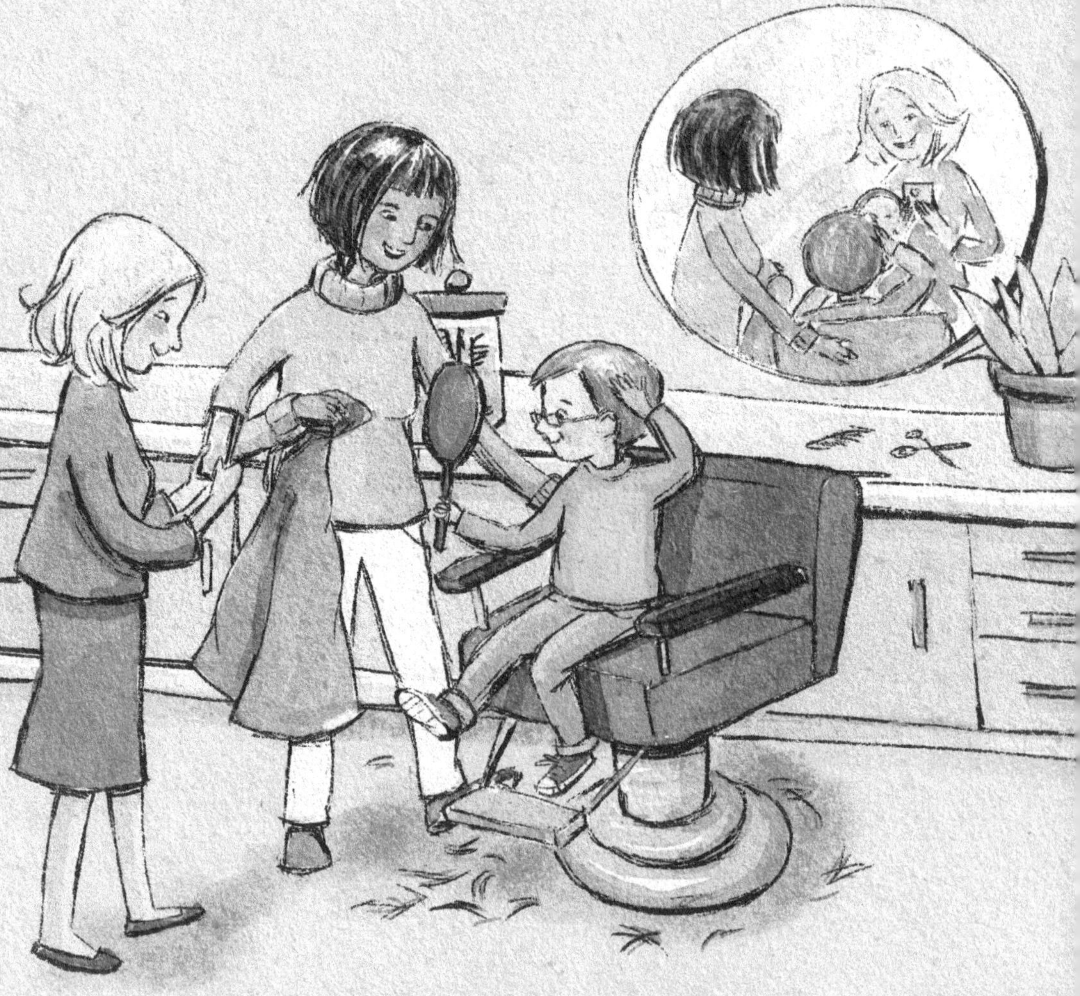

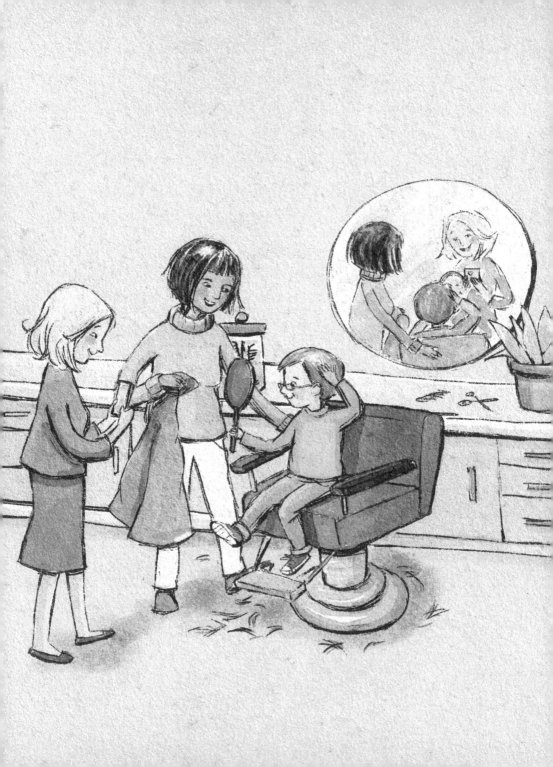

HAIRCUT

AGE 6

I'm not sure I had ever been so excited about going to an appointment in my entire life, much less a haircut appointment, but there I was sitting as far on the edge of my seat as my seatbelt would allow as Mom slowly pulled into a parking spot at the salon.

The day before, Mom had made a last-minute decision to stop by a walk-in haircut place. She wanted us to get fresh trims since school was starting later that week.

"Mom?" I asked. "Can I cut my hair short? Like a boy?"

I held up a magazine that had been sitting in the lobby and showed her a grinning boy about my age with his hair cut short on the sides and a bit longer on the top. My own hair fell just below my chin, so it wasn't overly long. But it definitely didn't look like a "boy" haircut.

I had asked her this question a few times over the years and she always seemed hesitant. I think it was because she was scared that people would mistake me for a boy, and she worried that would make me feel bad. What she didn't know yet was that it would have made me feel good to have people recognize me as a boy.

This time she hesitated again, but then knelt down next to me and looked closely at the picture. "You know what I think?" she started. "I think we should take some time looking at a few more pictures to make sure you find a style you really like. Then we can make an appointment to get it done at Dad's salon tomorrow." I agreed and we all shuffled out without the trims.

Later that day, we spent some time with Dad looking at pictures of boy hairstyles and I found a couple that I thought would look really cool on me. Dad thought so too. "You still won't look as fly as me," he joked.

"I know. I'll look better," I answered, grinning.

As I lay in bed that night, I pictured myself with my new haircut. I woke up early the next day and Gabby was up and excited too. She had also decided to change her hairstyle this year, but definitely not like how mine would be. We may be identical twins, but we haven't had the same hairstyle since we were, like, two years old.

"Remember, tell her to trim just a little off mine," Ellie said (over and over) as we loaded into the minivan. She was trying to grow her hair long, so she wasn't happy about the idea of getting it cut.

Once we parked, Mom turned to me and asked, "Are you sure about this?"

"I'm sure," I said. "It's just hair. If I don't like it, it will grow back." I added this last part to calm her nerves, because I was more than sure about this haircut. Beyond sure.

When we got inside, a friendly lady greeted us and called my name first. She put one of those cushion things under me 'cause I was really short. Then she threw the cape thing over me and buttoned it in the back.

"So, what are we doing with your hair today?" she asked, smiling.

I glanced at Mom and she nodded. "I want to cut it short, like a boy's hair," I told the lady. Mom showed her the pictures for reference. I might have said some things during the haircut itself, but I don't remember because I was too excited and nervous to pay much attention.

Once the stylist was done with the haircut, she took off the cape thing and handed me a mirror so I could see the front and the back.

"Well? What do you think?" she asked.

What did I think? What did I think?!

It was AWESOME!

My new hair was really short and styled so my bangs were up kinda like a ski jump. It was just like the pictures I'd seen with Mom and Dad. It was not one of the short bobs that I'd gotten before that made me look more like a mini soccer mom than anything else.

Mom seemed to be lost in thought for a few moments before she pulled out her phone. "Wow, honey," she gasped. "It looks great. Say cheese!"

I couldn't hold back my smile.

Finally, I felt like I could see ME. The me I knew inside now matched the me others saw on the outside. I'd never felt that confident before when I looked in the mirror, that's for sure!

As we pulled into our driveway, I proudly announced to our neighbors who were sitting on their porch, "I just got a haircut!" Me shouting out a window wasn't typical, but my haircut was too cool not to share.

"Oh, you went short like Tinkerbell," the makeup-and-dresses neighbor called to me.

TINKERBELL?! Try Adam Levine!

But I was too happy to argue. My sisters and I went inside and played house. This time I was the prince. According to six-year-old me, short hair = prince.

About a month later it was school picture day and I was super excited. I didn't wear anything special and I forgot to smile. When we got our picture packages, Mom asked, "Do you want to do retakes? You're not even smiling."

"No way!" I answered. That was my favorite school picture for a looong time.

I might not have been smiling in the photo, but I was smiling inside for sure!

WHICH LINE?

AGE 6

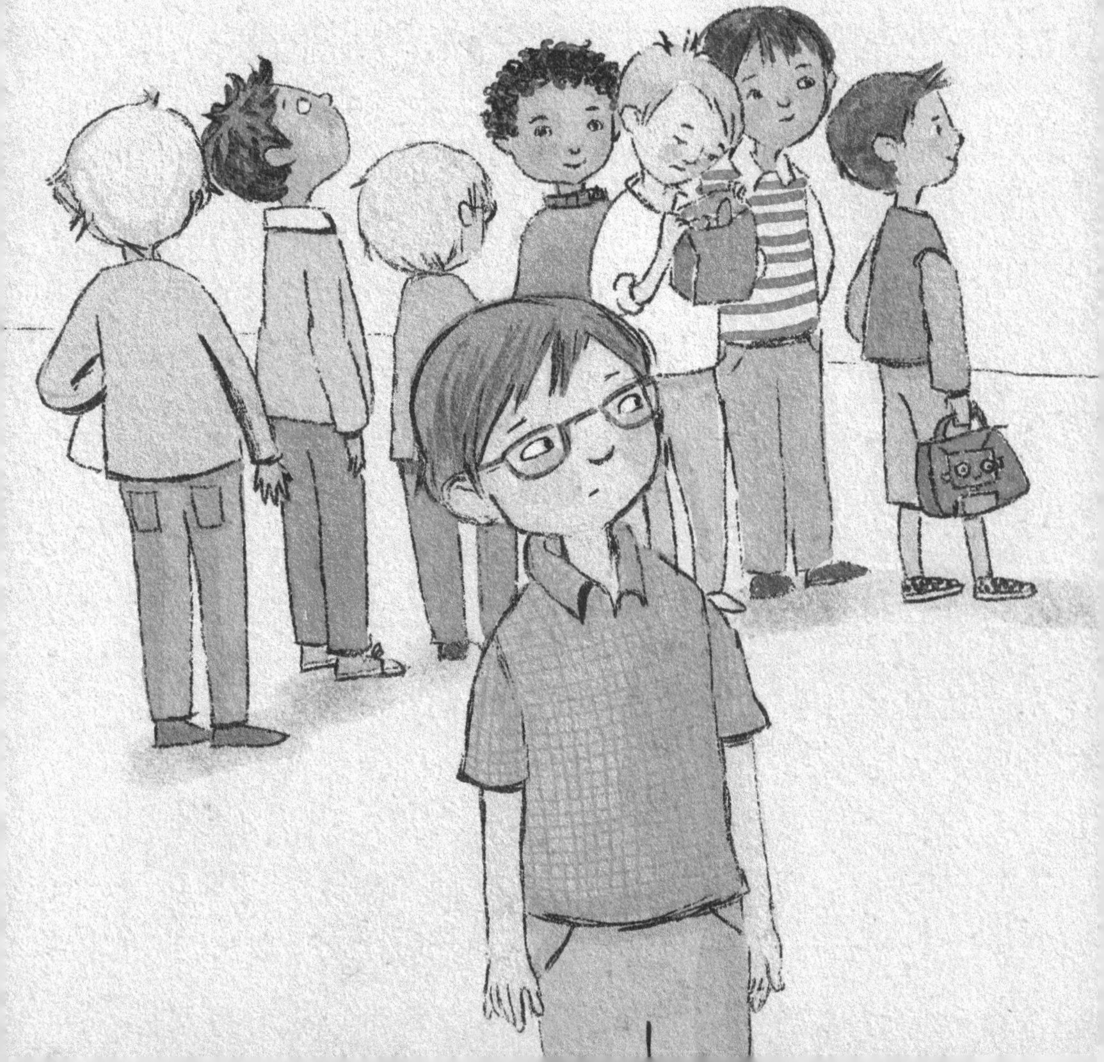

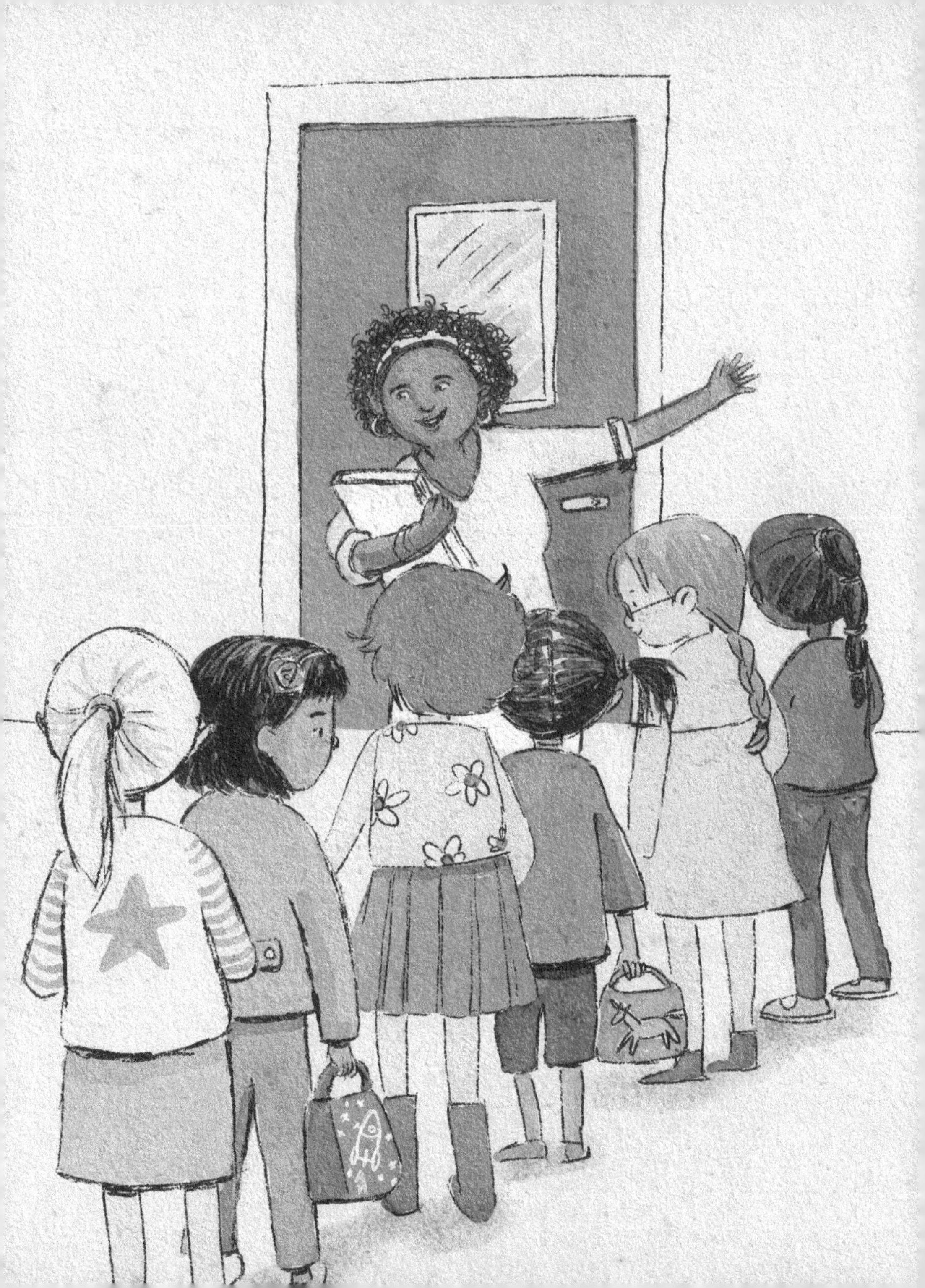

"Good morning, sweetheart! You up yet?" Mom called.

"Yes, I'm up!" I yelled back.

I had been up for an hour. I was so excited.

I hopped out of bed and looked in the mirror. I was looking good. The day before I had finally gotten my hair cut short like a boy. I put on a new short-sleeved button-up shirt and some khaki pants, then slung my brand-new Spider-Man backpack over my shoulders.

I was all ready to start first grade!

Well, as ready as I was going to be. I wasn't sure how the other kids would react to a girl with short hair and wearing boy clothes.

I got off the bus and walked to the blacktop where classes always gathered on the first day of school. I was an old pro—I had already been to kindergarten. I found my class's line and got in. At first, I was nervous that we would have to pass by the fifth graders (scary!). Luckily, they headed toward the school first. The day was off to a great start.

Inside my new classroom, our teacher, Mrs. Wahl, let us explore our very own desks (in kindergarten we shared tables), then asked us to come sit on the carpet where we sang a few songs that I found a bit babyish for us big first graders.

"Now, boys and girls, we're going to practice going through the lunch line in the cafeteria," said Mrs. Wahl. "Boys line up here and girls line up over there."

Uh-oh. Where should I go? I started to feel butterflies in my stomach as kids began to assemble into lines.

My heart wanted me to go in the boys' line. But I had spent six years being told I was a girl and used a girl's name and she/her pronouns. I took my best guess and stepped into line.

"Um, this is the girls' line," one of the girls informed me.

I nodded. "Yeah, I know." A few other kids looked at me funny.

"But you're not a girl!" she continued, like I really should have known that. I guess I didn't realize how much my haircut and clothes made me look like a boy.

"Um, I am in the right line," I mumbled quietly. Part of me wanted to agree with her and join the boys. I wasn't in the right line. But like I said, I had always been told I was a girl.

"Zoe is a girl, actually," Mrs. Wahl said, trying to rescue me. (Oh, I should let you know that Zoe was my old name, also known as my "dead" name.)

"Oh." The girl shrugged, seemingly satisfied that nobody was breaking the rules.

And that was the end of that.

Except for the awkward feeling that stuck with me for the rest of the day. And the question that stuck in my mind:

Which line SHOULD I be in???

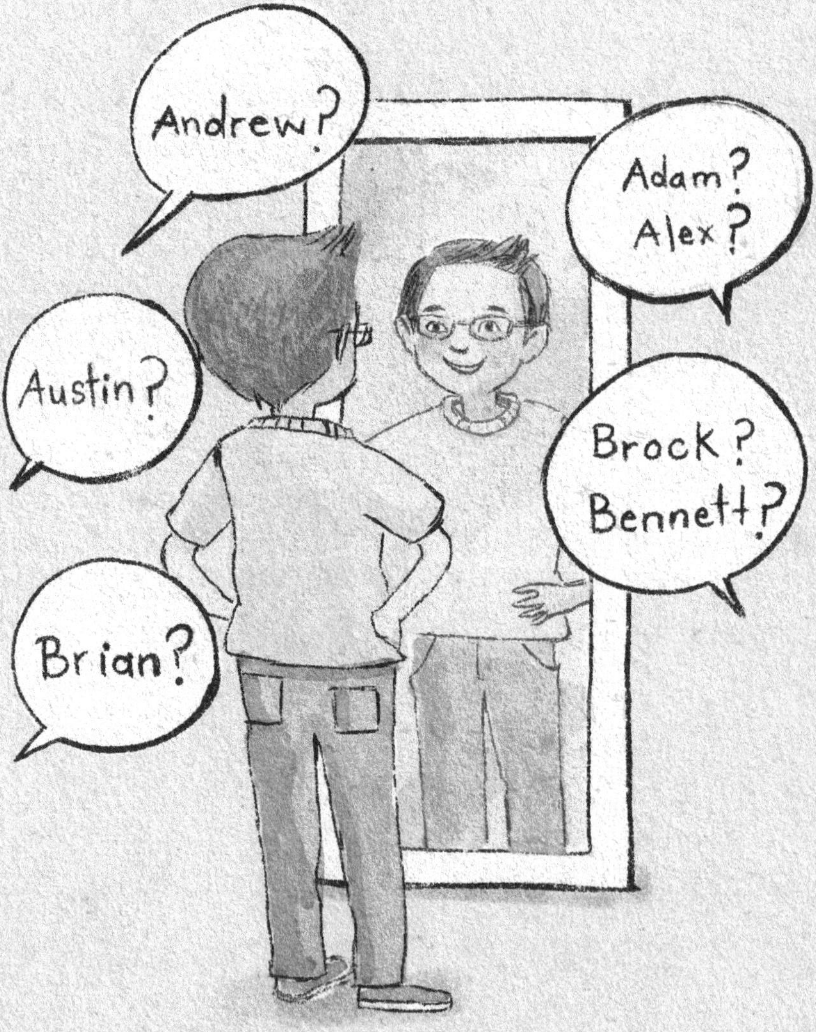
Andrew?
Adam?
Alex?
Austin?
Brock?
Bennett?
Brian?

A BOY NAMED ???
AGE 7

After one particularly difficult day at school, Mom sat next to me at bedtime and asked, "How was your day?"

"Pretty good, I guess."

"You guess?"

"It just feels like every day someone asks me if I am a boy or a girl. I'm not sure how to answer them. I don't feel like they are asking to be mean. It's just that...

I look like a boy.

I have short hair like a boy.

I dress like a boy.

But...

My name is Zoe.

And I use 'she' pronouns.

I can't really blame them for being confused!"

Mom sat quietly for a moment, then asked, "Why don't you tell people that you feel like a boy in your heart and your mind?"

"Because that would be cheesy. And it doesn't feel like the truth. I don't feel like a boy...

I AM a boy."

I was a boy. I very clearly knew and had always known that I was a boy inside. But I also understood that I wasn't a boy in everyone else's eyes. I was supposed to be a girl because of the body I was born into.

After what felt like a very long time, my mom looked me in my eyes and said, "Sweetie, if you are a boy, then you shouldn't have to be called 'she' any longer. It's possible for you to change your name and to go by 'he.' How would that feel?"

Her words filled me with hope and joy.

I had known for a while that changing my name and pronouns was possible, but up until that moment I'd had a hard time imagining how my family and friends would react to it. I also worried that if I changed my pronouns, I would no longer be my sister's "identical twin." I wasn't sure how I felt about that or how she would feel about it. But mostly, I had just been too nervous to do anything about it.

Until now.

"Um... that would feel AWESOME!" I said, my worries melting away as soon as Mom told me it was a real option. "I don't want to be called 'she' anymore. And I am ready to change my name... TOMORROW!" As the idea took hold, I could barely contain my excitement. "Can you email Mrs. Raplinger and tell her? Tonight?"

"Whoa whoa, honey, slow down." Mom smiled. "I promise I'll talk to your teacher, but it will probably take a little while before you can make the change officially. Why don't we start by talking to Dad and your sisters? And you should think about what your new name will be."

Oh, that's right. I had to choose a new name for myself.

For a long time, I liked my old pirate name "Luke." But that didn't feel right anymore. I got out of bed and stood in front of my full-length mirror. I really looked at myself, which was not something I usually enjoyed. This was my chance to choose a name that really fit me. The real me. A name I would go by for the rest of my life.

What name suited me?

As I stared at my reflection, my mom rattled off various options starting with the letter A. "Adam, Alex, Andrew, Austin..." Then she moved on to B. "Brian, Brock, Bennett..."

"Grayson!" I blurted out. "I feel like a Grayson." I was talking to my mom, but also to myself.

"Wow," Mom said, looking at my reflection. "I love that name for you. How about Grayson Lee? You could share your dad's middle name."

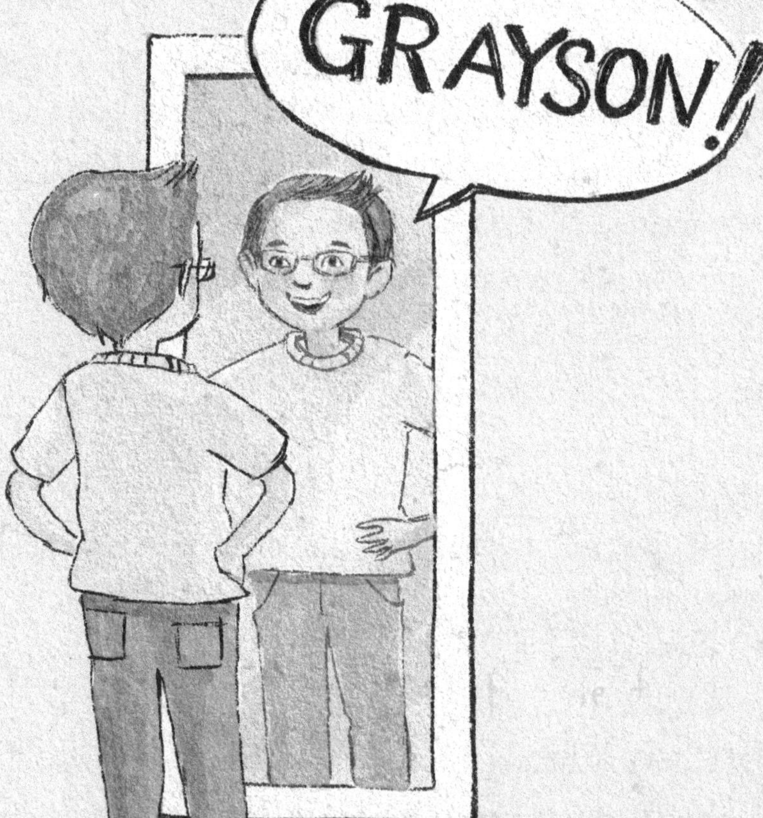
GRAYSON!

"Grayson Lee it is!" I said happily. "Let's go see what the family thinks."

Of course the rest of my family already knew of my feelings about being a boy, but me being ready to change my name was news.

"I think it really suits you... Grayson," Dad said. "You're ready for this, aren't you?" He wrapped his arm around me and gave my shoulder a squeeze. "Just make sure you tell me how to spell it."

"Gabby and Grayson. Grayson and Gabby. It has a nice ring to it," Gabby said, writing our twin names out on a piece of paper. "It's going to be hard getting used to calling you a new name, but you've always seemed more like a 'he' to me, so I'm sure it won't take me long."

"Yay!" Ellie cheered, "I like Grayson! Now I have a big sister AND a big brother!"

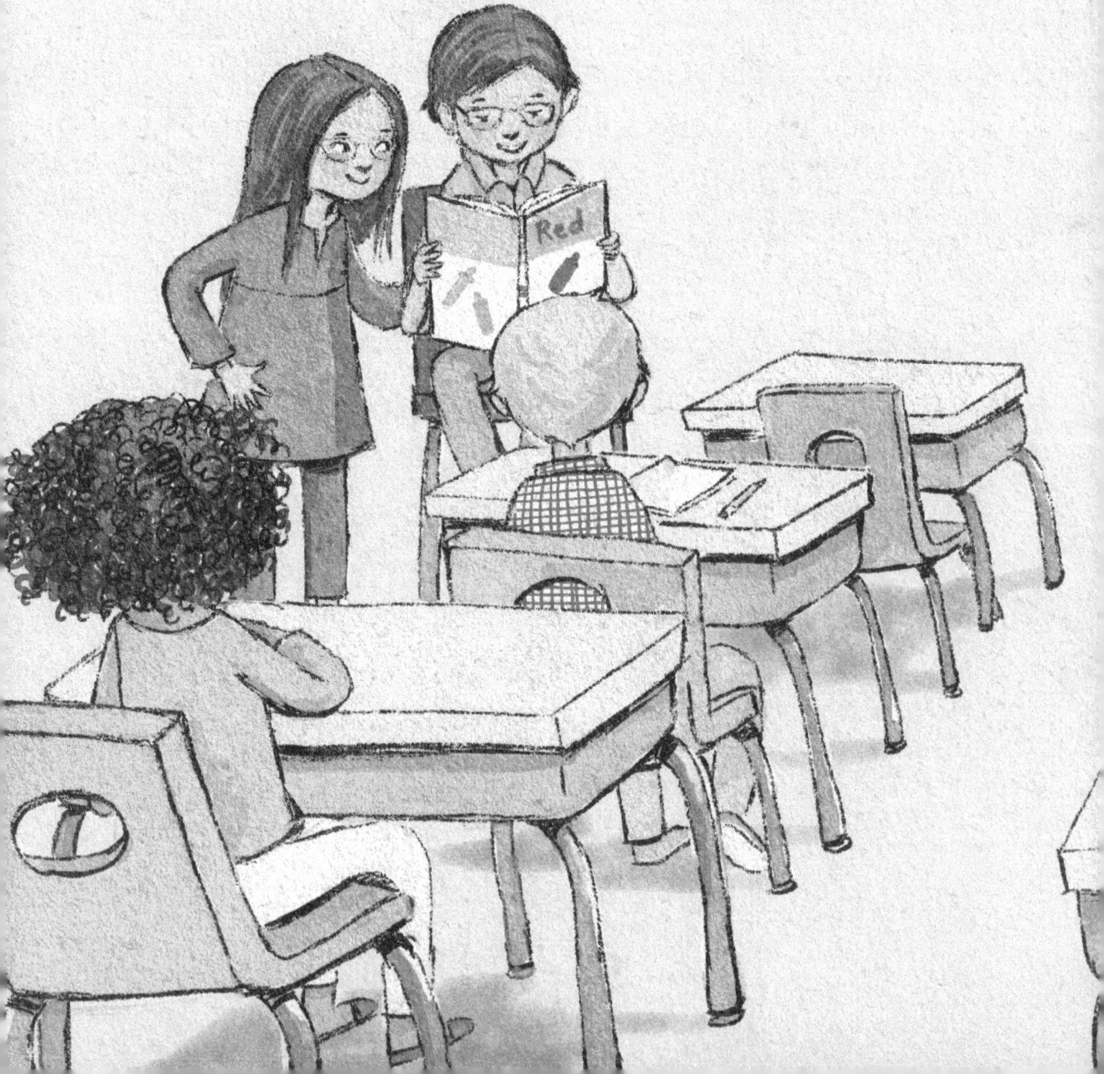
Red

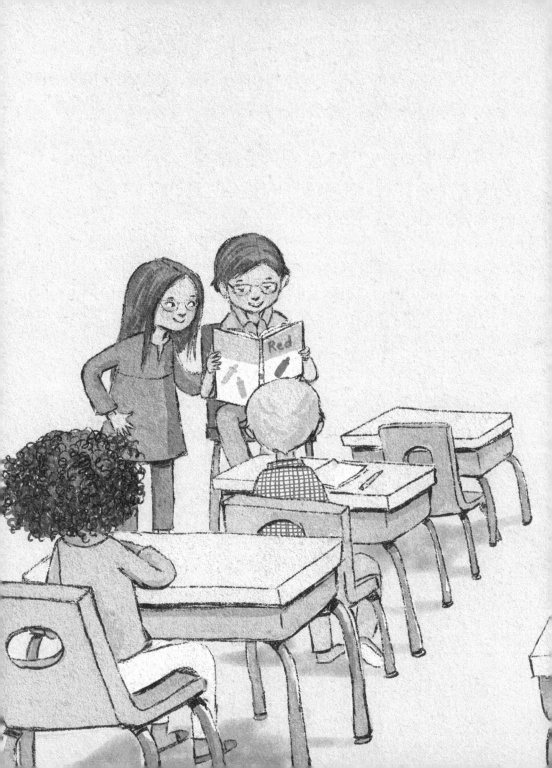

THE SPEECH

AGE 7

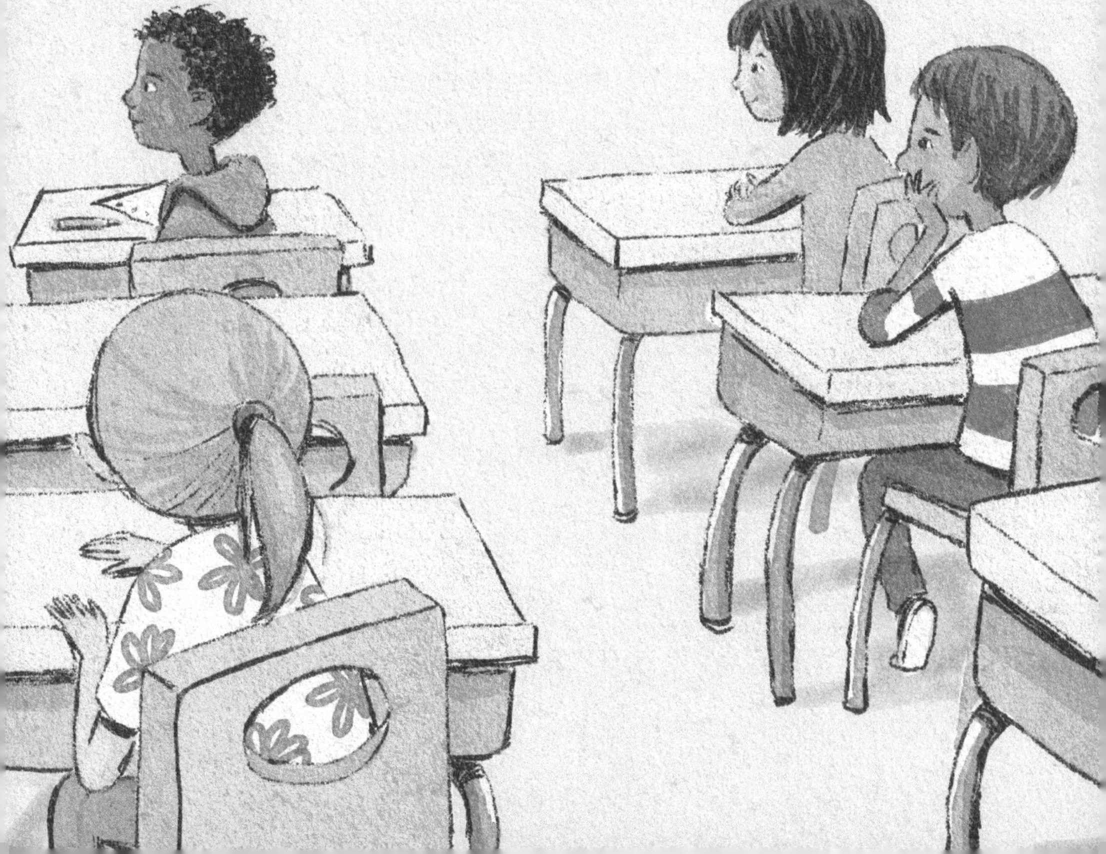

My knee was bouncing nervously under my desk and I could feel sweat on my palms. I was dressed up and ready, but I'm not gonna lie—I wasn't paying much attention to the teacher until she called our names.

"Grayson. Gabby."

Just a few days before, I had finally made the decision to change my name and pronouns, and now here I was, ready to share the news with my entire class.

Luckily, I had Gabby by my side.

Though I'd wanted to be called "he" for as long as I could remember, I had always planned to wait until middle school to make the switch.

But by second grade, someone asked me if I was a boy or a girl nearly every day. I couldn't wait until middle school—that was years away. I was tired of not knowing how to answer their questions.

"Grayson and Gabby have something to share with you," Mrs. Raplinger announced.

As Gabby and I walked to the front of the room, our classmates looked at each other in confusion. They'd never heard the name Grayson before. Mrs. Raplinger had pulled over a tall chair for me to sit in. I felt important, even though my feet didn't touch the ground, because it was one of those important teacher chairs. Gabby stood beside me.

I pulled out the sheet of wrinkled paper: the script I had written out the night before. Mrs. Raplinger nodded and I took a deep breath and began to read.

"I know you all think of me as Zoe, but I don't feel like a Zoe. I have decided to change my name to Grayson. I know it may be hard for you to remember my new name, but I need all of you to be supportive. I know some of you will make mistakes, but that's okay with me as long as you try your best. This may be hard to get used to, but eventually you will get it. Now I will read a book that shows my feelings. I hope you will enjoy it."

My hands were still shaking as I folded the paper up and began reading aloud from one of my family's favorite books, *Red*. It's about a crayon that has the wrong label and it can't do amazing work until the other crayons could see it for what it truly is. As I read each page, I turned the pictures toward the class the way teachers do to make sure all the kids can see.

When I finished, Gabby unfolded her own piece of notebook paper and read:

"My sister changed her name from Zoe to Grayson. She is now going by he. I know it will be confusing and not easy for some people, including me. I am sure there will be some people who forget now and then. That's okay. I forget all the time, but I try my best to remember and everyone else should too. At home, if we say Zoe instead of Grayson, we have to put a quarter in a special jar and Grayson gets to keep all the money. I hope everyone understands and will try their best to remember Grayson's name."

I really appreciated Gabby asking everyone to support me and letting them know it was okay to make some mistakes along the way. I knew it wasn't going to be easy. Looking back, my speech was kind of cringy, but I think the book and Gabby's speech helped get the message across to my classmates.

"Does anyone have any questions?" Mrs. Raplinger asked.

Just one girl raised her hand. "I feel shiny... can I change my name to Penny?"

That was it. Nobody else had any questions or much else to say. Later one of my friends told me that when I gave my speech he felt like he was going to cry and wasn't sure why. But he and I, like most of my other friends, stayed pretty close all through elementary school.

Over the next few weeks of school, everyone (including Mrs. Raplinger) tried their best to remember my new name. And they usually did. Occasionally they forgot, but I didn't really mind. People got used to it pretty quickly, and then it was just a regular thing.

It felt really good to finally be called by a name that actually fit me.

But I do kinda wish I had suggested using the quarter jar at school.

I would have made some bank that first couple weeks.

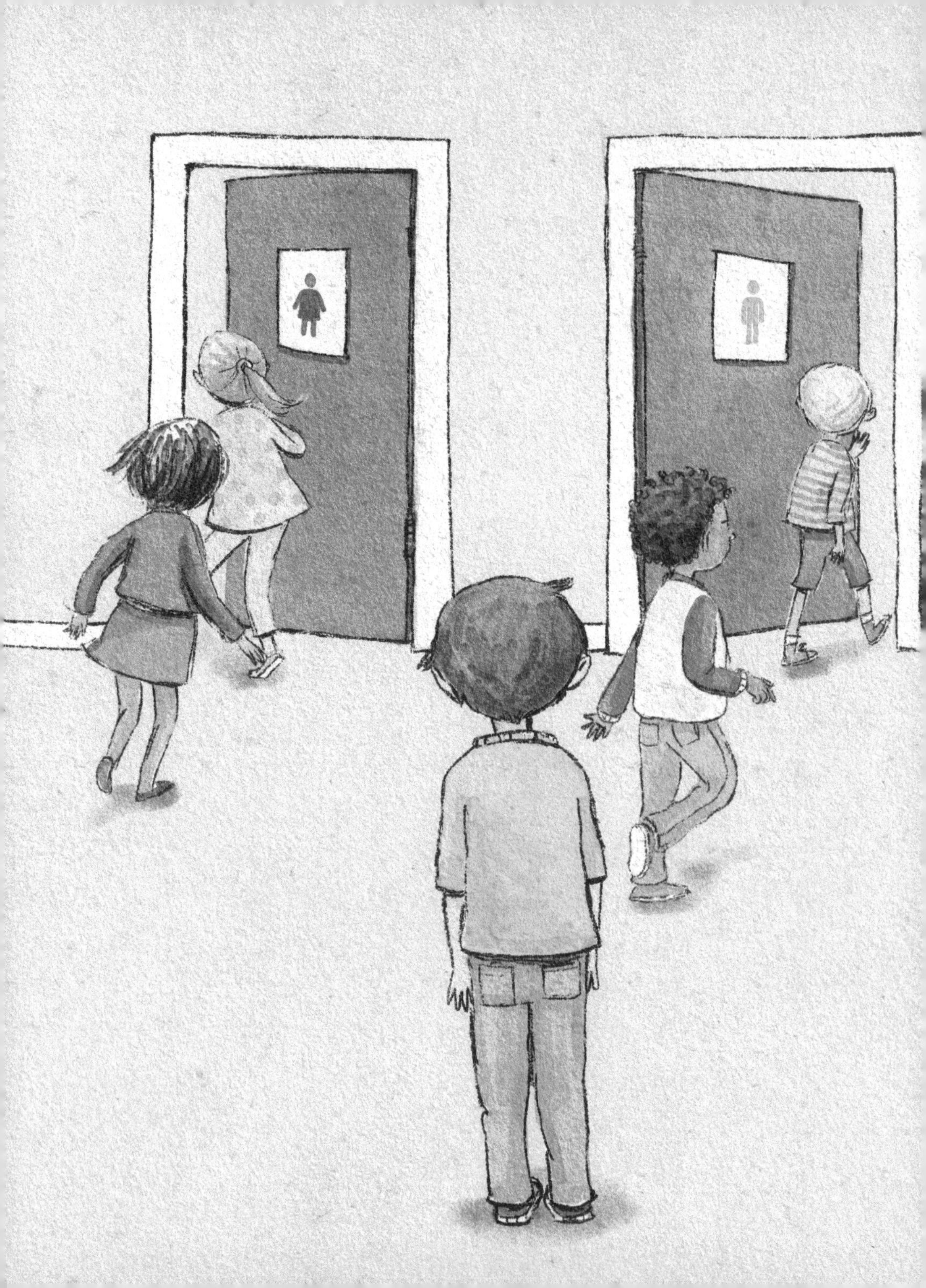

IT'S JUST A BATHROOM

AGE 7–8

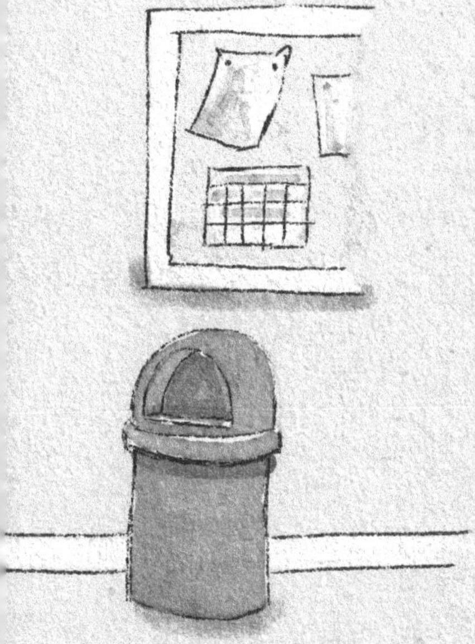

For most kids in school, going to the bathroom is no big deal. You raise your hand or grab a bathroom pass, you look for the boy or girl sign on the door before you go in, then you do your business and you're done. But for transgender kids like me, going to the bathroom can feel like a recurring nightmare. One particular instance that sticks out was in first grade...

"Can I go to the bathroom?" I asked Mrs. Wahl. I really had to go.

"Sure," she said.

I rushed to the girls' bathroom, holding an embarrassing pink pass. When I got inside, I realized a couple other girls were coming in behind me, so I hid in the stall, lifting my feet up so I'd be invisible.

I felt panicked. By this time I had my cool short hairstyle and looked just like a boy. But I was in the girls' bathroom. If I didn't know these particular girls, I would have to explain the situation, and how would I do that?

Suddenly, even more girls poured in—a whole group!

I was trapped.

If I left now and they saw me, I would have to deal with lots of confusion and embarrassing questions. And worst of all... giggling.

NOBODY likes to be laughed at, and that's a fact!

After that, I started avoiding the school bathroom at all costs. If I skipped the drinking fountain and only took a few sips of my milk at lunch and walked home after school really, really fast, I could usually make it to the bathroom the second I flew in the door.

It wasn't easy, but I managed.

"Mom, can you fill up my water bottle?" Gabby asked one morning as she rushed to get her shoes on to make the bus.

"Sure. Grayson, do you want me to fill yours up too?" Mom asked.

"No thanks. If I drink too much I'll have to go to the bathroom at school," I admitted.

"Wait... what? You're not using the school bathroom all day?" Mom asked, looking upset. I ran out the door without answering but could tell I'd have to explain when I got home. And I was right. After school I raced through the door and straight into the bathroom. When I came out, Mom was waiting.

"So what's going on with the school bathrooms?" she asked.

I stared at my feet. "I don't like using them."

"Why not?"

"Kids are always telling me I'm in the wrong bathroom. I don't know what to say, so I just hide in a stall until the bathroom is empty. It's just easier not to use them at all."

The very next day, Mom called Mrs. Wahl who suggested I use the staff bathroom that was right outside our classroom. I mostly still held it until after school, but it was a good solution for first grade.

Second grade was a different story...

Now don't get me wrong, second grade was great (maybe my all-time favorite year in school so far). But the bathroom situation really sucked. My second-grade teacher, Mrs. Raplinger, was okay with me using the staff bathroom, but the bathroom for second-grade teachers was not right outside our classroom.

It was in a busy area that was always full of kids. Also, it had a giant "Staff Only" sign on the door, reminding students they were not allowed inside.

Although I had special permission, I felt weird every time I used this bathroom. Kids who didn't know me (and some who did) loved to inform me of the rules by pounding on the door, rattling the handle, and yelling for all to hear:

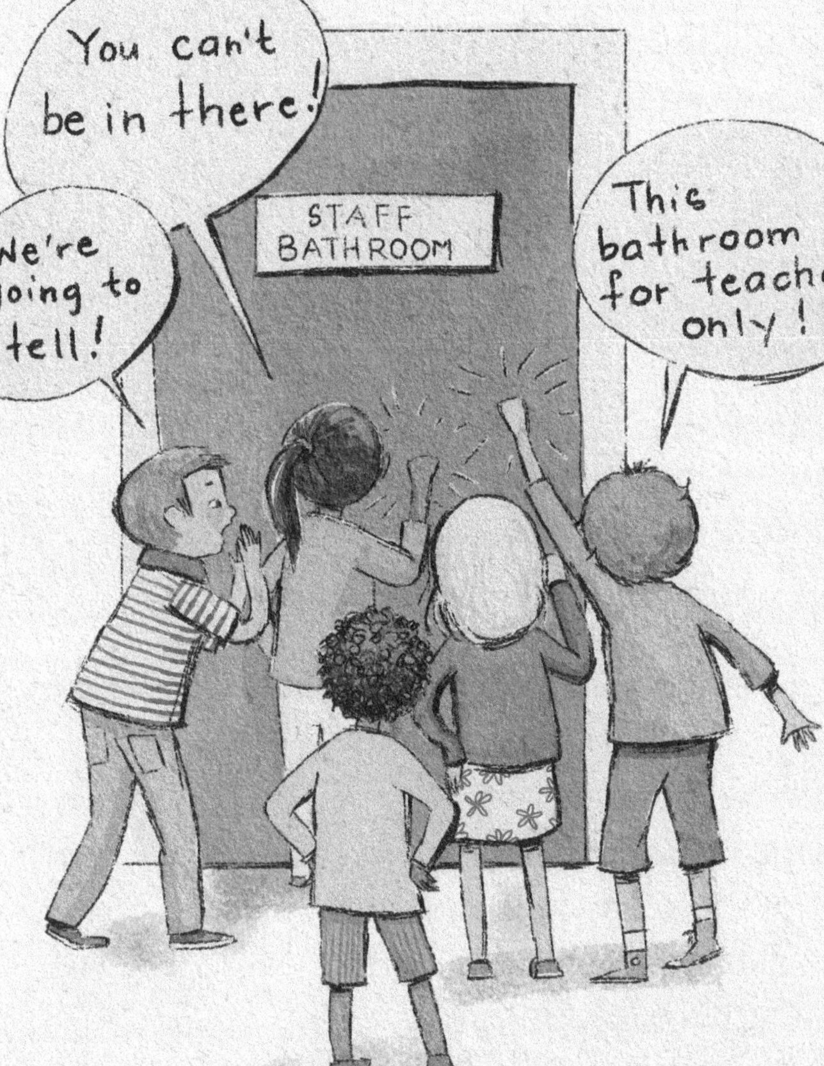
You can't be in there!
We're going to tell!
STAFF BATHROOM
This bathroom is for teachers only!

I had no idea how to respond. If there is one thing I really don't like, it's having attention centered on me. Especially when I don't know what to say. I was actually afraid they might try to stop me from going into the bathroom, and then I'd have something even more embarrassing to deal with... WET PANTS!!

No matter how badly I had to go, the sound of kids knocking on the door and the fear that they might yank it open made it not only hard to go, but extremely uncomfortable. As you can probably imagine.

On the rare times when there were no kids around and I could use the bathroom in peace...

"HALLELUJAH!"

Before leaving this bathroom, I always pushed open the lock as quietly as I could and peeked out to make sure the coast was clear. Just like in the first grade, I soon got tired of this and decided it was easier just to hold it until I got home.

Eventually, I shared my new bathroom challenges with my mom. "I just want to use the boys' bathroom," I told her in frustration. "Everyone knows me as Grayson now."

Mom talked it over with Mrs. Raplinger and they decided that using the boys' bathroom might make some of my classmates uncomfortable and they didn't want me to have to deal with more awkward questions. They decided I could use the nurse's bathroom for the rest of second grade. (My mom still regrets not pushing harder for the boys' room.)

I wasn't too excited about this idea because it meant I'd be the odd one out again. Although it worked out better than I expected, second-grade me wished I didn't have to worry so much about something as basic as going to the bathroom. I just wanted to use the boys' bathroom... like any other boy.

Is that too much to ask?!

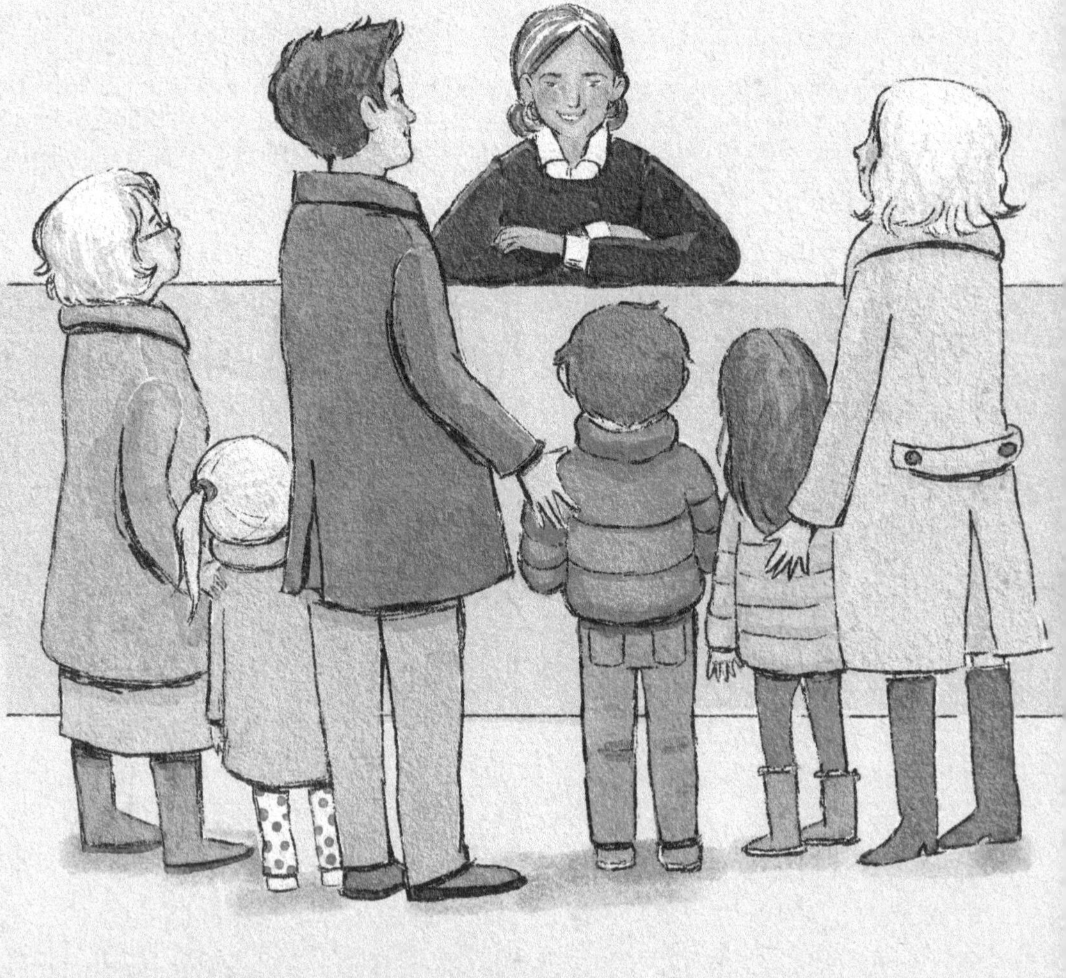

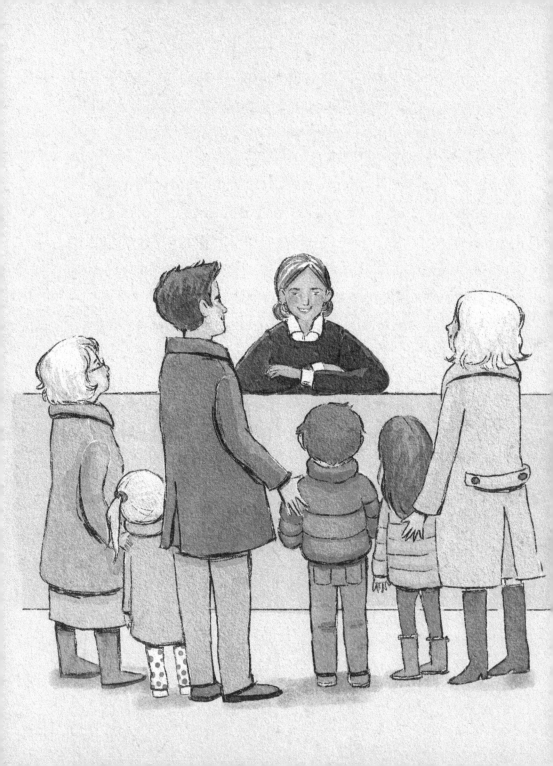

MY DAY IN COURT

AGE 8

Today's the day! I thought as I opened my eyes.

Last night I had carefully set my alarm for seven in the morning. I wanted to get up early so I would have plenty of time to get ready. Today I was going to court to legally change my name.

Guess I was pretty excited. I woke up at six a.m.!

Even though it was still dark outside, I hopped out of bed and started getting ready. I put on a nice shirt and some dress pants. I grabbed my dad's hair gel and styled my hair. I smiled BIG in the mirror.

"Ooh, snazzy!" Mom said when I walked into my parents' room to see what they thought. Dad was barely awake. I walked into Gabby's room, and it turned out she was also getting ready. Well, if you think getting ready is doing her hair and then redoing it because one strand of hair wasn't absolutely perfect. My little sister was still snoring as loud as ever.

Soon, though, we were all up and going. We ate breakfast together, which we don't do much, and all of us were in a good mood. Normally, we would have to go to school right now!

I was kinda annoyed because it was freezing outside and I had to put a hat on over my styled hair. Oh well. First stop was picking up my grandma. She was coming to be an additional witness to testify that my parents weren't forcing me to change my name or something. I was just glad she would be there with us.

Once we got to the courthouse, we went through security then into the courtroom. (Side note: I took off my hat and to my surprise, my hair looked even better!) We sat down but had to wait awhile because there was a lot of traffic and the judge was late.

That gave me plenty of time to worry about all the ways this could go wrong.

What if the judge doesn't like the name I picked?

What if she is like my neighbor and thinks it's wrong for me to want to be a boy?

What if she never shows up and I can't get my name changed?

My brain spun with questions.

Finally, she showed up and we got started. I don't remember much about the proceedings, mostly because it was really boring. What I do remember is the judge asking me a few questions like:

"Is this your family here with you today?"

"Do you want to change your name?"

"Do you want to be a boy?"

I answered yes to all.

I must have missed her hitting the gavel on that wooden thing, but next thing I knew they were handing us copies of the court documents approving my new name and my birth certificate with a gender change to "male."

Seeing my new name and with "male" next to it in print sent joy all through my body.

Grandma offered to take us to lunch to celebrate. Then I had to go back to school. But I didn't even mind. I had a great joke planned.

"Hey, where have you been?" my friends asked when I got to class late.

"Court," I answered.

"Court?! What for?" they asked, surprised.

"I robbed a bank!"

I got a few laughs and I smiled the whole rest of the day. It's wild how something as bland and boring as sitting in court answering a judge's questions had such a huge impact on me.

In the best way.

DOCTOR VISITS

AGE 8

BEEP BEEP BEEP...

I opened my eyes to the annoying racket of my alarm clock. I dragged myself out of bed and slowly got dressed.

Unlike my day in court, today wasn't going to be a super fun day. Today I had to go to the doctor. To get a shot. And I hated getting shots.

I REALLY hated getting shots.

Doctor visits are something I've gotten pretty used to. I've had a lot over the years. Starting at age six, I've had therapy visits every few months to help me make sure I'm really transgender and that it's not "just a phase."

Starting at age seven, I've also had appointments with an endocrinologist (thank you, autocorrect!) named Dr. Emerson. These appointments are only once or twice a year and I don't mind them because they usually just x-ray my hand to see if my bone growth is where it should be for my age. (And I still secretly like the cheesy toys they give me when I'm done.)

Not all trans kids see endocrinologists, but my mom was worried (of course) about my bones getting weaker, a possible a side effect of the medicine. She wanted someone paying close attention to my bones before I started getting Lupron shots.

Endocrinologist
↓

Lupron is the hormone blocker medicine that would hit the pause button on puberty for me. I didn't like the idea that I'd be pausing puberty while Gabby and all my friends moved ahead, but the alternative was developing boobs and a more "girly" body.

Way worse than shots!

As we headed up the elevator from the parking garage, Mom told me, "Don't forget, we're in lot four!" I made it my mission to remember so she would be impressed.

She checked us in at the office and then we sat in the waiting room. While we waited, a nurse put some numbing cream on the place where they'll do the shot. Before we discovered this cream, I sort of freaked out about shots. Thanks to the miracle numbing cream, I handle them better now.

Then we waited.

Finally, a nurse took us to the endocrinologist's office, where we waited some more. Dr. Emerson finally arrived and did what she always does. First, she asked me:

"Does everything feel normal?" (Yes.)

"Do you feel safe at home?" (Yes. But this always feels like a strange question.)

Then my least favorite question:

"Shall we see if your chest is developing?" (Um... do I have a choice?)

Then Dr. Emerson felt my chest to see if I was developing yet. The chest development tells the doctor if I've started puberty and can begin blocking the hormones that come with it.

I'm sure all this chest development business is for a good reason, but I didn't like having to wait... at all!

I am usually pretty quiet at the endocrinologist appointments, but my mom asks A LOT of questions (surprise, surprise). Dr. Emerson always takes time to answer *all* of Mom's questions. I pretend not to be interested, but I'm actually listening to every word.

"How long will he take the blockers?" was Mom's first question.

"Likely he'll take Lupron for about two years," Dr. Emerson answered.

"What side effects should we watch for?"

"Sometimes Lupron can impact bone density. Some kids start puberty as early as nine and have to start blockers then. Hopefully, Grayson will start puberty later so he'll take Lupron for less time. That will be easier on his bones."

(Luckily, I did start later, when I was twelve).

"When will he start taking testosterone?" Yet another question from Mom.

"Most likely when he's around fourteen. I'm not sure exactly when, but we'll keep checking his hormone levels and bone growth so we can maximize his growth potential."

"Maximize growth potential" means balancing my hormones in a way that will give me the most time to grow. I don't fully understand all the details, but I think once your body has a certain amount of estrogen or testosterone, your growth stops. Dr. Emerson will help me get the right amounts so I can grow for as long as possible. I am already pretty short for my age, so I'll take any help I can get in that department.

The shots I'd been getting for years were not yet hormone blockers *or* testosterone. They were just blood draws to gauge when it would be time for me to start those.

Basically, I was getting a shot to see when I would be ready to get some other shots.

Did I mention that I hate getting shots?

But I wasn't in a terrible mood on this day, believe it or not. Even though I hated getting shots, I knew the outcome would be good for me. Going through female puberty was the worst thing I could imagine happening. It's going to be bad enough living with my sisters as they go through it. I do think it might be weird as people around me have growth spurts and I don't. Especially Gabby—she better not get taller than me!

And I was really excited about taking testosterone, eventually. That will lower my voice and might help me grow some facial hair, just like other boys when they go through puberty.

After answering every single Mom question, Dr. Emerson sent us down to the dungeon to get the shot. By that time, the numbing cream was working, so I knew I wouldn't feel it. But that didn't stop me from panicking a little. My heart raced as I avoided looking at the needle that was penetrating my skin.

"Done," the nurse said.

What? I hadn't felt a thing!

Finished with what felt like shot #498, Mom and I headed home.

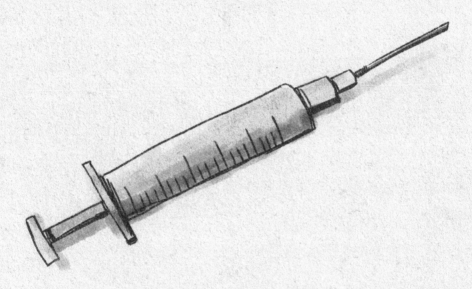

P.S. I totally forgot we were in lot four.

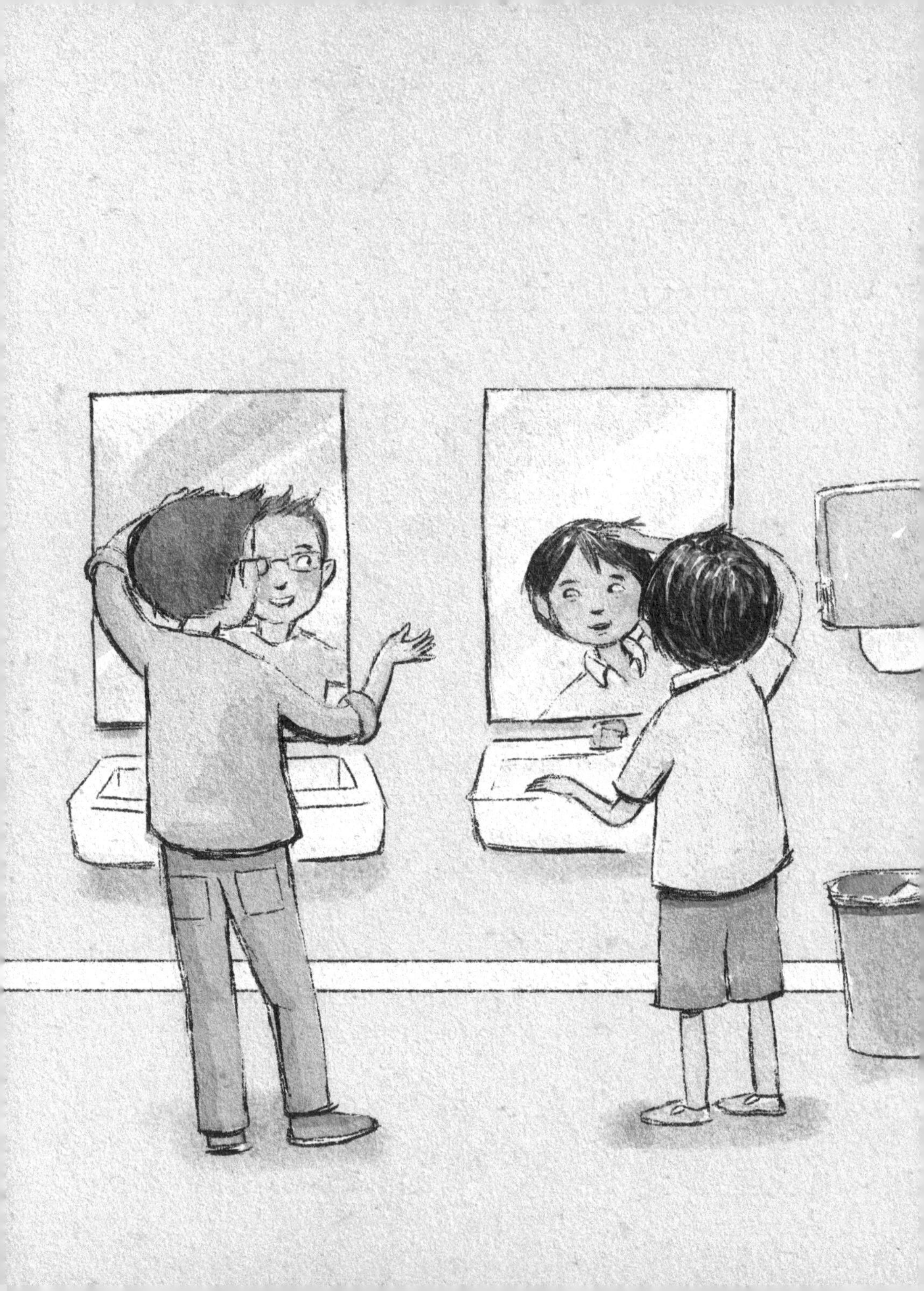

COMING OUT...
AGAIN
AGE 8

Once third grade rolled around, there were more kids in my class who hadn't known me before I transitioned. I made some new friends that year and they only knew me as Grayson. In some ways, that was good, but in some ways it was bad.

"When should I tell them that I'm transgender?" I asked my mom. "What if they don't want to be my friends anymore?"

"Then they aren't very good friends," she answered.

I guess I didn't look satisfied with that because she followed up with "You don't have to tell them if you don't want to, you know."

I did know that, but I figured if I wanted to have a good friendship, then I should be honest. I decided to tell my new friends the next day. If they didn't like it, then they didn't have to be my friends.

The first conversation was pretty easy, despite my awkwardness. I was in the boys' bathroom with my friend Aaron. We were both looking in the mirror and combing our hair back with our hands.

"Uh, do you know what transgender means?" I asked.

"Yeah..." Aaron answered.

"Okay... well... um... I'm that," I sputtered. "Like, trans. Transgender. I'm transgender, I mean."

I know—so smooth, right?

"Oh, uh, okay, cool," he said, shrugging like it was no big deal.

PHEW!

The second conversation with my new friend Randy was a little different.

"Do you know what transgender means?" I asked Randy, while we were eating lunch.

"Um, no."

"Okay... uh... okay, well, it's like... um... when you're born as a girl but, like, not really 'cause you're always a boy in your head, but then you change from looking like a girl and being called a girl to looking like a boy and being called a boy."

"Oh."

"And it can be the other way around too."

"Cool?"

"And, um, I'm that. The first thing."

That made me panic a little. I didn't know if I should say yes or no. My mom told me that when people asked that question I could say, "I've always been a boy in my head" or "I've always been a boy in my heart." But I didn't want to sound too cheesy with my new friend.

"Yep, pretty much," I replied.

He didn't believe me and kept asking me if I really used to be a girl. Every chance he got. For the next week.

It was annoying. Very annoying.

Eventually, Randy got used to the idea and we continued to play video games together after school, and he kept asking me to be his partner in class. But I couldn't forget his reaction.

It bothered me so much, I wrote a note about it which I hid under my pillow. When I eventually let my mom read it one night, she looked like she might cry. Instead, she gave me a big hug and rubbed my back a little longer than usual.

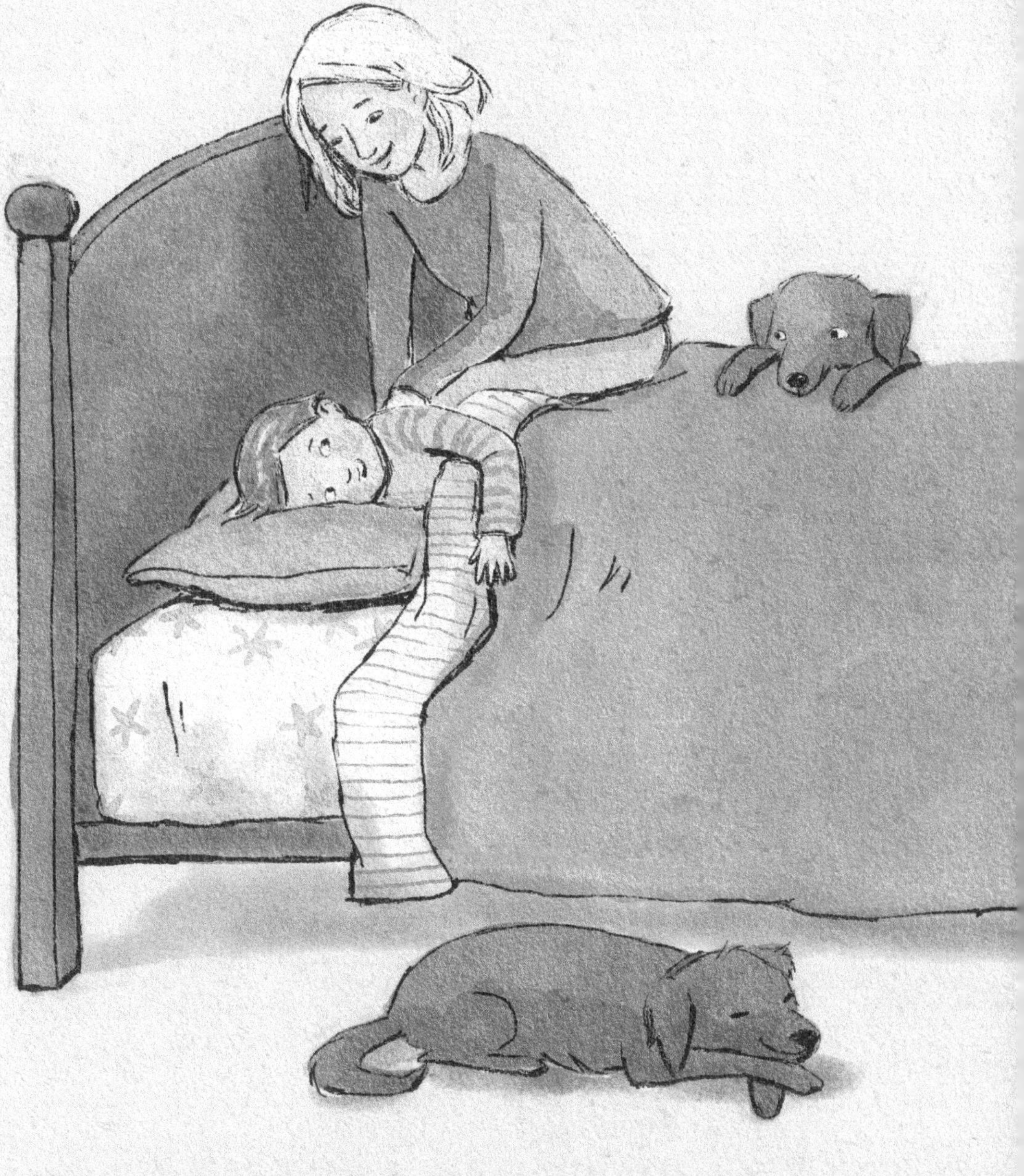

WHAT IF
THEY HAD SAID NO?
AGE 12

I don't remember getting more than seventy-five cents from Gabby in the quarter jar, so I guess she got used to my new name pretty quickly. My whole family did, actually. We went to a family wedding in Mexico just two weeks after I decided to change my name. Everyone tried really hard to call me Grayson and use my new "he" pronouns. Occasionally, they made mistakes, but mostly they got it right and kept telling me how proud they were of me.

I didn't really understand what I had done that was so brave.

I was just being me.

Gabby has always been one of my strongest supporters. She not only stood by my side during our second-grade speeches, but she always notices the smallest things that might make me feel like I don't belong. Like the first Christmas after my name change, she hid my old stocking with "Zoe" on it and reminded my mom to hurry and order a new one with my correct name.

When people used my "dead" name, it was a constant reminder that I didn't feel like I belonged. I felt the same way every time people called me "she" instead of "he." So when Gabby realized we didn't yet have ornaments with my new name on them, she quickly made a few homemade ones to hang on the tree.

Throughout school, she has shielded me from a lot. When people are curious or have questions about me, they often go ask her. I'm sure that has been uncomfortable for her.

Yeah, she's a pretty great sister (don't tell her I said that).

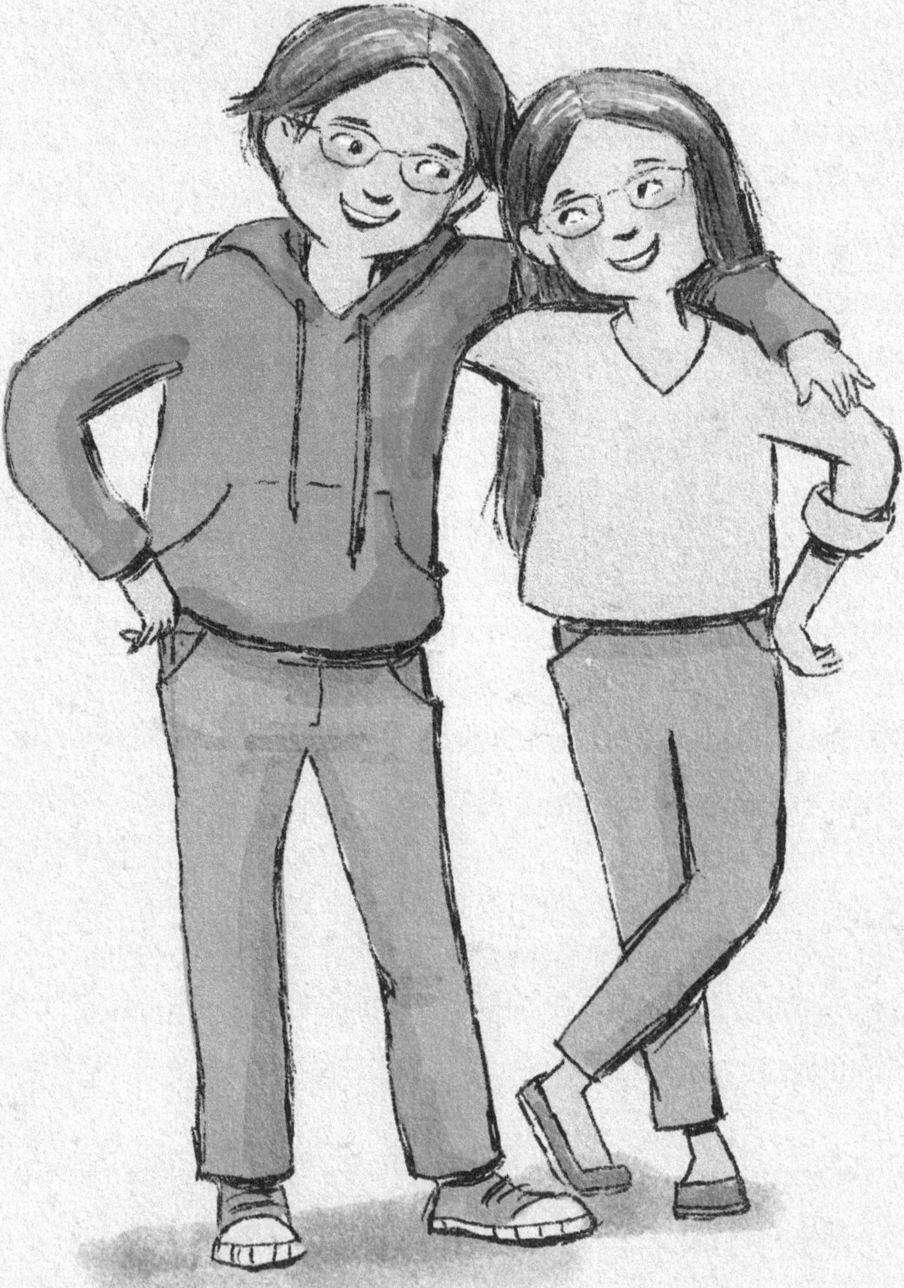

More recently, she has spent a lot of time reading and learning about what it means to be transgender and LGBTQ+. She helps other people understand it better and can be surprisingly bold when she sees something that might be offensive or harmful to me or anyone else in the community.

I am so glad that despite my gender identity, we still consider ourselves "identical" twins. My younger sister Ellie is supportive too. Sometimes I wonder if she even remembers that I wasn't born a boy biologically—she was really young when I changed my name and pronouns. At least she never makes me feel like she remembers, which is great!

Fast-forward to today—it's been over five years since I changed my name and pronouns. I am officially Grayson Lee White with "male" accurately listed on my birth certificate. Most people see me as "he," even those who knew me before my transition. I have to say, all of these changes have made me so much happier and more confident in general.

Don't get me wrong, I can be socially awkward. And I'm still pretty shy and introverted, especially around people I don't know. But I no longer feel like what people see when they look at me is different from who I know myself to be.

I don't have a huge group of friends, but the ones I have are good friends. They like me and accept me for who I am. They support me and I am very comfortable around them. Although I sometimes feel a little jealous about things they can take for granted—like being able to pee standing up or not having to take medicine to avoid growing boobs—we like similar things. Playing video games, skateboarding, riding our bikes, and of course snowboarding! We have a lot of fun together.

When I meet new people, it's hard to decide when and if I should share the fact that I am transgender. It can be uncomfortable talking about it, especially as I get older and am dealing with puberty. Being transgender is a big part of my identity for sure, and something I am not at all ashamed of. But it's just one part of my identity. I am also a gamer, an author, a snowboarder, a golfer, a brother, a friend, and a DOT SON.

I'm glad I changed my name when I was young because I've discovered kids get more judgy as they get older. My classmates in elementary school hadn't really learned to be biased yet, so they were very open and accepting of my transition. As I've gotten older, people have started feeling the need to share how they feel about transgender people, or more specifically, how their parents feel about them. Whenever somebody says to me, "I have a question," or "Can I ask you something?" I get nervous. I'm scared they will ask me something that leads to an awkward answer, or an answer they won't understand or won't agree with.

But there's one thing about my transition I don't even like to think about... what if Mom hadn't told me that changing my name was an option?

Or worse... what if I had suggested it and my family had said no?

I'm really lucky that didn't happen and that I've always been accepted by my parents, siblings, grandparents, friends, our dogs... and pretty much everyone else in my life. Aside from the many uncomfortable moments and curious questions, most people I know have been supportive and kind to me during my transition.

I know how lucky I am. I know there are lots of other kids who are trans like me, who don't get that kind of support from their family and friends, and I feel terrible for them.

If I didn't have that support, I would still be trapped in the wrong body.

How would that feel?

I don't even like to think about it.

AND LET'S END
AT THE END
AGE 13

"Just do it. No countdown," I said to the nurse.

A second later I felt a small prick in my leg and then an ache, like when you move a sore muscle.

"That's it!" the nurse said cheerfully. I had officially started taking hormone blockers!

My mom smiled. "Great job, Grayson."

I hadn't really done anything to deserve the praise, but y'know, I appreciated it.

Because it hasn't been all easy for me. I've had a lot of challenges related to being transgender. A lot of:

doctor appointments

therapy appointments

court visits

bathroom disasters

awkward questions

awkward conversations

awkward tutus

and so many shots!

It's funny to think about how many years I worried about getting these blocker shots. It was a topic that came up with my therapist a lot. And in the end, the shots barely even hurt (especially with the miracle numbing cream).

Is it possible I have conquered one of my fears?!
One down, about a million to go. I am still plenty
worried about:

My twin sister Gabby growing taller than me.
Or worse, Ellie!

The hormone blockers not working and going through
female puberty.

Sharing the boys' locker room at school.

Telling someone I really like that I am trans—what if
they lose interest in me?

People not being able to get past my transgender
identity to really see me.

Having my own family someday.

Being lonely.

Not belonging.

But, as with my fear of shots, I've learned that many of my fears don't come true. So instead of focusing on my worries, I am going to stay focused on all of the great things in my life, like my awesome supportive family, my really great friends, and of course my two beautiful golden retrievers.

I will worry about worrisome things when and if they actually happen.

And even though my gender transition has been long and challenging, and there are things about the future that I worry about, I don't think I would change a thing about it. It has all been worth it to be myself.

Dotson.

Grayson.

Me.

GRAYSON'S GLOSSARY

Here are some words that would have been helpful to know as I was transitioning. Some are my own definitions and some I had to look up. Keep in mind that you are sure to hear and want to learn about other terms that aren't on this list. I learn new terms and things about being trans almost every day!

affirmed gender: a person's true gender, as opposed to their gender assigned at birth

assigned sex at birth: when you're designated as boy or girl based on your biology or body parts you are born with. This assignment can be incorrect as your gender identity is determined in your brain, not by your biological parts.

AFAB (assigned female at birth): when you were born, doctors announced "It's a girl" based on your body parts (in my case, the doctor was wrong!)

AMAB (assigned male at birth): when you were born, doctors announced "It's a boy" based on your body parts

cisgender: when your gender identity (how you feel) is the same as what doctors/midwives assigned to you when you were born (girl/boy or sex assigned at birth)

cross-sex hormone therapy: taking the hormone that aligns with your gender identity (testosterone for male, estrogen for female) to help develop some of the secondary sex characteristics of that gender, like a deeper voice and facial hair for boys

dead name: the name that you were given at birth. For some, using that name makes them feel really uncomfortable once they've changed their name as part of their transition.

Dotson: my made-up term (a combination of "daughter" and "son") to help myself and others understand that I was transgender before I had an official word to describe myself

enby: it's how you pronounce the initials NB, for non-binary

endocrinologist: a doctor who can help ensure that people develop the physical characteristics of their affirmed gender

estrogen: the main hormone that starts female puberty and characteristics, like breasts and a higher voice

FTM (female-to-male): when someone is born biologically female, but their gender identity is male. A more accurate way to say this is AFAB—you were assigned female at birth, but you always had a male gender identity.

gender affirming: when others respect your gender by using the correct pronouns, name, etc. It feels so good!

gender dysphoria: the distress you feel when your body doesn't match the gender you know yourself to be

gender expansive: when people feel that the traditional ways of being a "boy" or "girl" don't fit them. They live their lives showing that there are many ways to be a girl, boy, both, or neither.

gender expression: the way people choose to show who they are to the world, like through their clothes or hairstyles. People might think that these things go with certain genders, but really you can't guess someone's gender or pronouns from how they look.

genderfluid: when you feel and express a more masculine gender sometimes and a more feminine gender at other times

gender identity: how you feel or know yourself to be in your brain. Girl, boy, both, or neither. Everyone has a gender identity.

gender non-conforming: when how you look, dress, or act doesn't align with expectations of the sex you were assigned at birth (for example: a boy wearing a dress or a girl with extra short hair)

genderqueer: a catch-all term for people with non-binary gender identities. The term "queer" can be considered derogatory, so it's best not to refer to someone this way unless they've asked you to.

gender role: the norms society has created for how girls and boys should behave, or society's assumptions about gender characteristics (for example: girls are better caretakers and boys are better athletes)

hormone blockers: medicine that blocks the hormones that begin puberty. Hormone blockers hit the pause button on puberty until transgender kids are ready to start cross-sex hormone therapy.

intersex: when people are born with bodies that are naturally different from what is traditionally considered female or male (this occurs in about 2% of babies born, about the same percentage as redheaded babies!)

LGBTQ+: lesbian, gay, bisexual, transgender, and queer or questioning. These are words used to describe someone's sexual orientation or gender identity. The plus sign (+) is so this acronym isn't thirty letters long, as that's what would be needed to cover all the ways people identify.

non-binary: people who do not feel like the words "girl" or "boy" fits them. They may feel like both or neither. They sometimes use pronouns such as "they", "them," and "theirs." Same as enby.

MTF (male-to-female): when someone is born biologically male, but their gender identity is female. A more accurate way to say this is AMAB—you were assigned male at birth, but you always had a female gender identity.

puberty: the time when your body begins to develop and change as you move from being a kid to an adult. For most kids, it's when girls develop breasts and boys start to look more like men. It was something I feared more than anything because I did NOT want to go through female puberty.

sex: your biology or the body parts you were born with

sexual orientation: who you love or are attracted to

testosterone: the main hormone that starts male puberty and characteristics, like facial hair and a deeper voice

transgender: when your gender identity (how you feel) is different from what doctors assigned to you when you were born (girl/boy or sex assigned at birth)

transition: when you change your gender characteristics to match your gender identity. Each person's transition might look different. For me, it was socially transitioning my name and pronouns, taking hormone blockers to prevent feminine puberty, and eventually taking testosterone. Who knows if I'll do anything more throughout my life, but some people choose to do sexual reassignment surgery (also called gender affirmation or confirmation surgery).

transphobia: when a person or group of people doesn't like someone or discriminates against them just because they are transgender

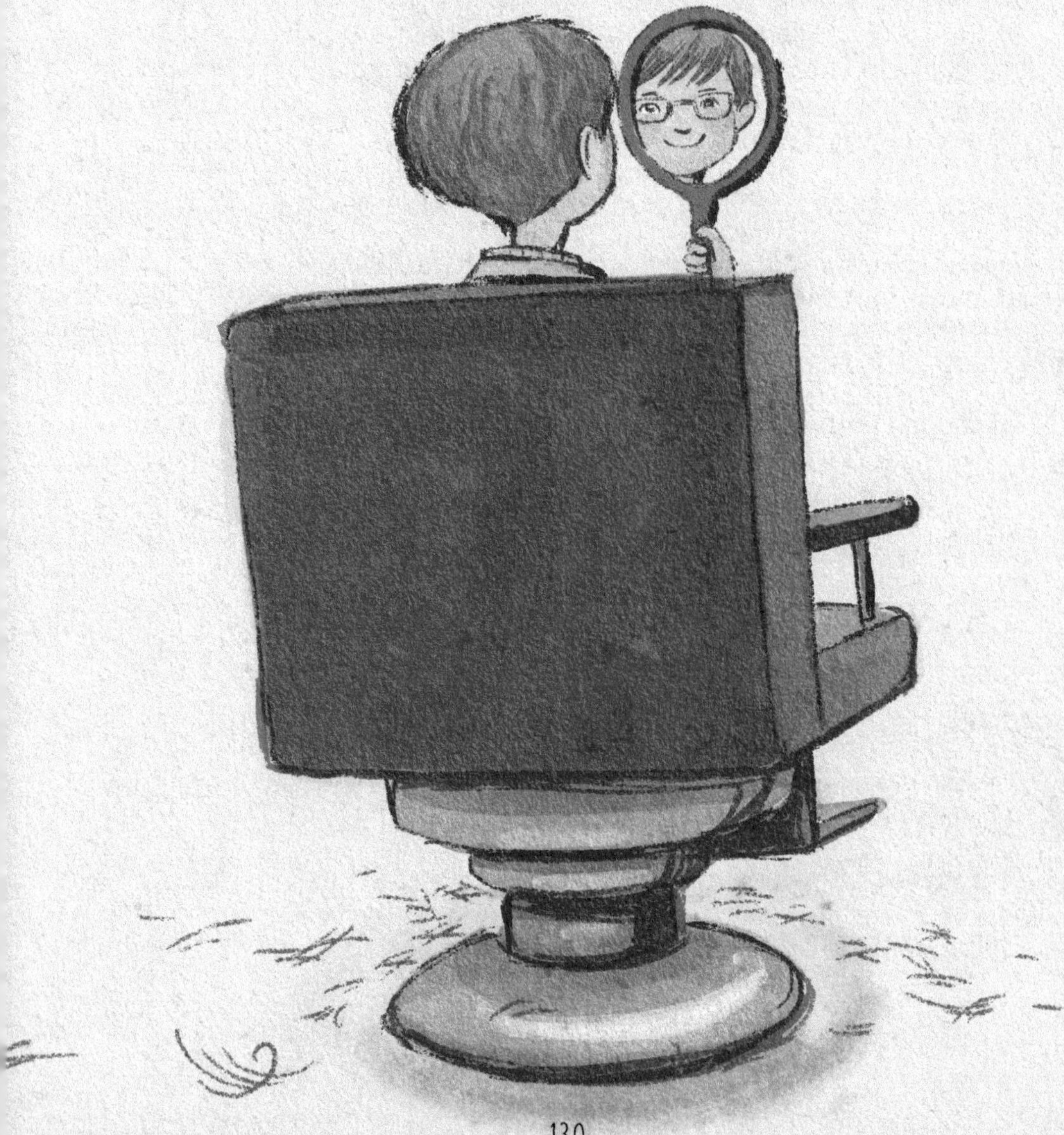

DISCUSSION QUESTIONS

Here are some questions that you can use to lead a discussion about the book! You may also come up with your own questions, and that's totally okay too! We just want to help you get the conversation started.

1. What did you like best about this book?

2. What did you like least or struggle the most with?

3. If you got a chance to ask the author of this book one questions, what would it be?

4. If you could hear the same story from another person's point of view, who would you choose?

5. What did you already know about this book's subject before you read this book?

6. Did you learn anything new that expanded or changed your perspective?

7. Why do you think the author chose to tell this story?

8. Which chapter stands out to you most and why?

9. What aspects of the author's story could you most relate to?

10. What do questions do you still have?

RESOURCES FOR TRANSGENDER KIDS & FAMILIES

Luckily, there are so many helpful resources out there now. Here are some that my mom says have been really helpful for her and our family. Check them out!

GenderCool
gendercool.org
Inspired by the experience of a transgender girl and her family, GenderCool is a worldwide movement working to increase visibility, understanding, and inclusion of trans people in books, ads, TV, movies, and more. It has also published some awesome books for kids.

Gender Spectrum
genderspectrum.org
This group works to create gender-sensitive and inclusive environments for all children and teens. It provides online programs, resources, and information for youth and families, and works with educators and others to increase gender understanding and inclusion.

Human Rights Campaign – Transgender Children & Youth
hrc.org/resources/transgender-children-and-youth-understanding-the-basics
This resource on the HRC website helps clarify the difference between "kids being kids" and kids asserting things that are critical to their identity and development—such as gender identity and expression.

National Center for Transgender Equality
transequality.org
This group is working to change policies and society to increase understanding and acceptance of transgender people—to replace disrespect, discrimination, and violence with empathy, opportunity, and justice. Its website has an especially helpful section on how to update your name and gender by state: transequality.org/documents

Trans Families
transfamilies.org
This organization supports transgender people and their families by running support groups, a trans youth leadership program, and more. Its focus is to build communities for families of gender diverse children.

Welcoming Schools
welcomingschools.org
A professional development program for elementary school educators on how to create LGBTQ+ and gender-inclusive schools, prevent bullying, and support transgender and non-binary students.

BOOKS

If you are interested in learning more and like to read as much as I do, these are some books our family recommends.

A Kids Book About Being Transgender, by Gia Parr in partnership with The GenderCool Project (A Kids Book About, 2021)

A Kids Book About Being Inclusive, by Ashton Mota & Rebekah Bruesehoff in partnership with The GenderCool Project (A Kids Book About, 2021)

A Kids Book About Being Non-Binary, by Hunter Chinn-Raicht in partnership with The GenderCool Project (A Kids Book About, 2021)

He's Always Been My Son: A Mother's Story About Raising Her Transgender Son, by Janna Barkin (Jessica Kingsley Publishers, 2017)

Raising Ryland: Our Story of Parenting a Transgender Child with No Strings Attached, by Hillary Whittington (HarperCollins Publishers, 2016)

Red: A Crayon's Story, by Michael Hall (Greenwillow Books, 2015)

The Transgender Child and The Transgender Teen, by Stephanie A. Brill (Cleis Press, 2008 & 2016)

SUPPORT HOTLINES

If you or a transgender person you know needs immediate support, call one of these hotlines and talk to a counselor.

Trans Lifeline
translifeline.org
(877) 565-8860
This trans-led organization provides a hotline and microgrants that give direct emotional and financial support to trans people in crisis.

The Trevor Project
thetrevorproject.org
(866) 488-7386
The leading national organization providing crisis intervention and suicide prevention services to LGBTQ+ young people ages 13–24. Youth can connect with a crisis counselor by phone, chat, or text.

ACKNOWLEDGMENTS

I feel really lucky to have been able to work with so many great people who helped turn my stories into an actual book. I'd like to give a special thank you to Target for believing in me as a young author and making *Dotson* a reality. Kate, I really appreciated how much you went out of your way to make me feel comfortable during our meetings and always made sure I was asked for my thoughts, ideas, or opinions on all details, no matter how big or small. I liked the fun ways you helped the team get to know me and for me to get to know the team. Jen, thank you for walking my mom and me through all of the important things to know about publishing a book and referring to me as an author right from the start. It made me feel pretty important. Also, thank you for finding Michelle to be my writing coach. I couldn't have asked for a cooler person to work with (she even loves snowboarding!). Michelle, I know it took a lot of work to organize the flow of the book. Thank you for taking the time to do that and for making what could have been a kind of boring editing process so easy. Thanks to Rachel for paying such great attention to the kind of illustrator we were looking for. Stephanie is amazing! Stephanie, not sure how you do it, but you brought so many of my experiences to life on paper and also had some really helpful recommendations. Olivia, thanks for making sure that all of the punctuation was right. I tried, but there were a lot of quotations. And finally, to my entire family, for loving me for me since day one; I appreciate you and know that my story is a happy one because of all of you.

Text © 2022 by Grayson Lee White
Illustrations © 2022 by Stephanie Roth Sisson

Edited by Michelle McCann

ISBN: 9781513141770

Printed in the United States of America
28 27 26 25 24 2 3 4 5 6

Published by West Margin Press®

WEST
MARGIN
PRESS

WestMarginPress.com

Proudly distributed by
Ingram Publisher Services